FOREWORD BY JEFF CLARK

FAITH
Living the Crucified Life

Ivan Q. Spencer

SELECTED & EDITED BY EDIE MOUREY

FURROW
PRESS

Printed in the United States of America
International Standard Book Number: 978-0-9800196-0-5

Publisher's Cataloging-in-Publication
Spencer, Ivan Q. (Ivan Quay), 1888-1970.
    Faith : living the crucified life / Ivan Q. Spencer ;
  selected and edited by Edie Mourey.
      p.   cm.
    Includes bibliographical references and index.
    ISBN-13: 978-0-9800196-0-5
    ISBN-10: 0-9800196-0-5

    1. Christian life—Pentecostal authors. 2. Spiritual life—Christianity.   I. Mourey, Edie. II. Title.

BV4501.3.S64 2008   248.4'8994
                          QBI07-600268

DEDICATION

This book is dedicated to Ruth Spencer Veach,
Ivan Q. Spencer's daughter and my mother.
Mom, I had no clue what had been in your heart for years
when GOD first dropped this project into my heart.
Apparently, it went "from your lips to GOD's ears."
And now, your father's words will be heard
by another generation.

ACKNOWLEDGEMENTS

Niswander is a family name long associated with Elim Bible Institute and with the watchful keeping of Elim's written treasury. And to that name—more specifically—to the name, Joy Niswander, I and all of Elim owe a great deal of thanks.

Joy, thank you for realizing several years ago how important the keeping of books was to our spiritual heritage. And thank you for guiding me through the wealth of resources.

Thank you, Jeff and Nancy Clark, my dear siblings who read with me the words of our grandfather. What a privilege has been ours! What an unmerited blessing we have received from our FATHER! Thank you for seeing this through with me.

Thank you, John Mourey, with all my heart and all my love. You have believed in CHRIST in me when I've doubted and feared. You are my partner, and I am glad you picked me to be on your team. You and Abbie have sacrificed some precious family time for the completion of this task. Thank you both.

Abbie, my girl, we have some treasured memories of trips made to Elim. Hopefully, these reminiscences forever have connected you to the place and the people I have been attached to since my birth—namely, to the oasis called Elim.

CONTENTS

EDITOR'S NOTE

Ivan Q. Spencer was a twentieth-century revivalist. Founder of Elim Bible Institute and Elim Fellowship of Lima, New York, he preached the life of faith, the soon return of JESUS CHRIST, and a last-days' outpouring in preparation for the LORD'S return. His was a consecrated life—a fully surrendered life—and he called disciples of CHRIST to follow their LORD'S example in laying down their lives and living the crucified life of faith.

While I was completing research in 1999 for *Elim—Living in the Flow*, I was struck by the amount of written teaching contained in *The Elim Pentecostal Herald*, the periodical published by Spencer and others of Elim. Many voices spoke on sundry subjects from the volumes of fatigued folios, but the one voice that I desired to know more intimately was that of my own grandfather, Ivan Q. Spencer.

I was two years of age when he died in 1970. I actually do not know if I have one authentic memory of him. The fact is I often was told of how he and I interacted in our two years of shared vulnerability—during my "toddlerhood" and his "senior-hood." But these stories could not define for me the spiritual father whose vision, work, and ministry have so widely impacted our globe and my world. And so, I found myself drawn to his writings in an effort to hear and know him for myself.

I discovered something else during my renewed research. I found that his words, though buried in a tome, could be educational and inspirational to yet another generation. And with this intent, I dusted the now discolored pages and collected the teachings herein under the topic of faith.

In essence, this book is both a compilation and derivative work, having additional text for organizational and transitional purposes. His chapter headings and their respective subheadings are mine in actuality, but their message is his message. The subsequent text is his with modifications so as to enhance the readability for today's audience.

I trust his words will speak to your heart and encourage you to follow CHRIST in faith, laying down your life in complete surrender to His will and to His call. In his own words, "Let go, and let GOD, for where you end, GOD begins."

— Edie Mourey

FOREWORD

I was never afforded the privilege of having met the man, I.
Q. Spencer. The message he carried and lived has made me
feel at times like I had known and walked with him. However,
I was privileged to walk with others who were close to him
and he to them, they having witnessed in him something to
be "downloaded" for theirs and ensuing generations.

I.Q. or "Pop Spencer," as he was known by those who
loved him, went to be with the LORD in 1970, six years before
I would step foot on Elim Bible Institute, the school that he
founded. By then, he already was considered a legend in
Elim's culture, having given himself wholly to the ministry of
preparing laborers for end-time revival ministry around the
world. He carried with him the distinct passion of bearing
and imparting the flame of the Pentecostal message, a message his generation dearly paid for so that our day would
know and experience its truths and impact in the world.

Having come from simple, hard-working stock, his lead-
ership was often mingled with many hours spent engaged in
tasks considered mundane to most, that of farming and
ensuring the school's small staff and its growing student body
would have food to eat. His message was walked out before
Elim's small community, a message of simple and yet pro-
found faith in GOD. Pop Spencer was confident in GOD's
desire to reveal Himself while proving His ability to provide
all that was necessary to walk with Him (or do His will) at

home and abroad.

Eventually, from Elim's small campus in upstate New York, thousands of laborers would be thrust into the harvest fields of the earth. This throng of servant-leaders would include missionaries, pastors, and Christian workers toiling in many different capacities throughout the nations.

Though Pop Spencer wrote proficiently, his writing was confined primarily to personal correspondence and *The Elim Pentecostal Herald*, Elim's bi-monthly periodical. When my sister-in-law, Edie Mourey, undertook the task of researching his writings chronicled in these publications, it became increasingly apparent that the most central theme running like a thread through it all was a riveting message of faith and living the crucified life. The marriage of the two might seem incongruous to some, as the concept of faith is certainly easier to grasp than the message of the cross. But to Elim's founder, these were inseparable concepts.

Our prayer is that this compilation of I.Q's writings on faith and living the crucified life will inspire and quicken in you, the postmodern reader, the same life-giving Spirit which Pop felt as he would traverse the Scripture and uncover its riches waiting to be seized by hungry seekers of any age. I am extremely thankful to Edie for making available the first of what I hope will be more of the writings of our founder, as we continue in these volatile days of global unrest to prepare a new generation of servant-leaders for harvest ministry worldwide.

— *Jeff Clark*
President, Elim Bible Institute

1

GOD'S WAY IS . . .

The Way of Faith

"'Oh, that My people would listen to Me,
that Israel would walk in My ways!'" (Psalm 81:13)

We read that JESUS said, "'Have faith in GOD'" (Mark 11:22). With this command, He directed His disciples toward both the Giver and the Substance of their faith. So if we want to know what faith is, we must go back to GOD and His ways. There we find GOD in His nature is faith, just the same as He is love, holiness, and every Divine characteristic in perfection. Our GOD is Faith! Our GOD is faithful, praise His name! All His activity, all His plans and purposes have been wrought and are still being produced on the basis of His eternal faith.

GOD spoke at the beginning, and it was done. He said, "'Let there be light'; and there was light" (Genesis 1:3). And how did He speak?

> ALL OF GOD'S EXPRESSIONS ARE EXPRESSIONS OF FAITH—POINTING US TO THE WAY OF FAITH.

He spoke in faith. All of GOD'S expressions are expressions of faith—pointing us to the way of faith. All His blessed Word is full of the expressions of the GOD of faithfulness. So this is just like all the other wonderful attributes of GOD, like all of His Divine characteristics.

Our GOD always works through this avenue of faith. As His children, we come to know Him and His ways, understand His actions, and actually get acquainted with Him through the way of faith. Abraham, Lot, Moses, and the children of Israel, all grappled with discovering the way. We know from reading the Scriptures that two of these found it while the others did not.

ABRAHAM AND LOT

The Scripture says, "By faith Abraham obeyed when he was called to go out to the place which he would receive as an inheritance. And he went out, not knowing where he was going" (Hebrews 11:8). He must have had some revelation from GOD. I think he had a revelation much further than most of us have, and I question whether most of us would be able to step out like he did in his day and follow the LORD, not knowing where we were going.

> A GREAT MANY OF GOD'S PEOPLE ARE WAITING FOR SOMEONE TO CARRY THEM THROUGH THEIR DIFFICULTIES.

In these days, it is not so hard and difficult to step out and go into a new place. It was different in Abraham's day. The fact of Abraham's leaving his family and household and separating himself meant a great deal, and it was no wonder Abraham only partially obeyed at first. He had to take his father and Lot along and stay in Haran, not leaving there until after his father died.

And Lot was quite a challenge for him. Yes, Lot always was getting Abraham in wrong. Lot means cover. He was always under cover. All that Lot ever was, he owed to Abraham's faith. A great many of GOD's people are waiting for someone to carry them through their difficulties. You can find a few faithful war horses today who know how to fight battles in faith. GOD, though, wants to bring us into the place where there will be a dependence upon Him that no matter which way the wind blows and what other people say or think —or what the circumstance and environment might be—we will walk on with Him just the same.

In spite of the challenges Lot presented, something happened, however, that became a pattern for Abraham's life of faith. Look at his life. You will find occasion after occasion when Abraham would have a vision of GOD—a revelation— that moved him out in the ways of GOD and in the life of faith.

On one particular day, the LORD Almighty appeared unto him and said, "'I am Almighty GOD; walk before Me and be blameless'" (Genesis 17:1). Almighty in Hebrew is *El Shaddai,* the All-sufficient One. How do you think that revelation touched him? Because he had a vision of GOD Almighty, he could walk before Him and be blameless; he could be perfect.

On another occasion, the angel of the LORD visited him. The revelation that Sarah should bear him a son in his old age was brought to his attention the second time. When Sarah heard it, she laughed. Here Abraham's faith was tested, yet the Scripture says he hoped against hope (Romans 4:18).

Abraham received this test and then another and, finally, another revelation of GOD. The ultimate test came when GOD told Abraham to come up into the mount, bring Isaac, and offer him as a burnt offering. This time, Abraham's faith moved him to act quickly. There was no partial obedience. It says, "So Abraham rose early in the morning" (Genesis 22:3). Faith can always rise up early to obey GOD, stepping right out upon a command of GOD, knowing that He is able.

> FAITH CAN ALWAYS RISE UP EARLY TO OBEY GOD, STEPPING RIGHT OUT UPON A COMMAND OF GOD, KNOWING THAT HE IS ABLE.

So Abraham obeyed in offering up Isaac, knowing GOD was able to raise him from the dead. In that testing, Abraham had a revelation. JESUS said, "'Your father Abraham rejoiced to see My day, and he saw it and was glad'" (John 8:56). Doubtless Abraham had a revelation of the plan of salvation. He saw down through the ages the glories that were to be revealed. He, as did Moses, knew GOD's way of faith and saw the Hope of his nation.

MOSES AND THE CHILDREN OF ISRAEL

Psalm 103:7 tells us, "He made known His ways to Moses, His acts to the children of Israel." Moses, like Abraham, became acquainted with GOD and His ways, but the children of Israel did not understand GOD's dealings with them. They only saw His acts and did not know His ways.

> SOME ONLY SEE THE ACTS OF GOD. SOME RECOGNIZE HIM IN MEASURE . . .

The children of GOD today are not too different from the children of Israel in Moses' day. Some only see the acts of GOD. Some recognize Him in measure, at least while He is about them and they see His doings, but yet they are not acquainted with His ways. And because of this, they never get to know the LORD intimately. They know not the secret of abiding in His Presence or of a continual fellowship, life, and ministry in the SPIRIT.

Moses, on the other hand, began to acquaint himself with GOD's ways. He was a prophet. He had the Word of the LORD —GOD's expression of faith. He saw the LORD, walked with Him, and had communion with Him. But it was said of the children of Israel, "'"They always go astray in their heart, and they have not known My ways"'" (Hebrews 3:10).

All those days when JEHOVAH led Israel like a shepherd

leading his flock out of Egypt, when He led them through the Red Sea and through the wilderness to Canaan and its possessions, all those miraculous steps were made by GOD. Israel, however, only saw what happened and did not understand the paths of GOD. The result was that her people wandered here and there, going astray, never knowing the secrets of His way.

There are many people who are going the same way today because they know not the ways of GOD. They are traveling according to their own dictates and not following His. These have not discovered yet that there is a vast difference between their ways and GOD's ways.

Isaiah says, "'For My thoughts are not your thoughts, nor are your ways My ways,' says the LORD. 'For as the heavens are higher than the earth, so are My ways higher than your ways, and My thoughts than your thoughts'" (Isaiah 55:8-9). The desire in our hearts above all others should be to search out His ways, to acquaint ourselves with them, to get into them, and to allow them to get into us. We must come out of our own ways and undergo a great inner work before we can know His.

HIS WAY

Generally speaking, the ways of GOD refer to His paths, His mode of life, and His doings. There are some paths GOD travels; He does not travel every path.

If you want to begin to know GOD's ways like Abraham and Moses did, you must get on the path He travels. In Psalm 84:5, we read, "Blessed is the man whose strength is in You, whose heart is set on pilgrimage [on a highway]." GOD has highways on which He travels. Are any of them in your heart?

> THERE ARE SOME PATHS GOD TRAVELS; HE DOES NOT TRAVEL EVERY PATH.

Psalm 77:19 reads, "Your way was in the sea, Your path in the great waters, and Your footsteps were not known." This section of the psalm speaks of two things which are very precious to me. First of all, it tells us something about where His way is—it's in the sea, the great waters. Secondly, it speaks to us of our being brought into a place of absolute helplessness in ourselves and absolute dependence upon Him. It is indeed a way of faith.

GOD HAS HIGHWAYS ON WHICH HE TRAVELS. ARE ANY OF THEM IN YOUR HEART?

Were you ever on the sea in a storm and saw how helpless you were? If we all could see this, we would realize how insignificant and helpless we actually are. If you ever get across a storm-tossed sea, it will be because GOD has undertaken for you.

I don't suppose Jonah realized this when he started out the opposite way from GOD's leadings. He didn't know GOD's path was in the sea. He found it out, though, before he went very far.

Paul on his way to Rome had this lesson, too. He had a call to Rome, and to Rome he had to go, and GOD's way was in the sea.

In the storm at sea, there was a landing place GOD provided; some went on boards and others on pieces of the ship. All this happened while Paul was going to Rome in the will of GOD.

Do you know what they did with the ship? It tells us that they loosed the rudder bands, thrust up the main sail, cast off the anchors, and let her drive (Acts 27:40). These four things they did. These four things we must do today: cast off those things holding us back, loosen our control over our lives, avail ourselves to GOD, and commit ourselves to His wind—all in faith. How important it is for us to yield up to the SPIRIT and let go and let GOD! We must come to our end, beloved, for where we end GOD begins. It is the only way we will ever become acquainted with His ways in the sea. All our natural ideas and ways must go to give place to GOD'S watery way.

> **WE MUST COME TO OUR END, BELOVED, FOR WHERE WE END GOD BEGINS.**

But there's yet another way of GOD that the psalmist mentioned when he wrote, "Your way, O GOD, is in the sanctuary" (Psalm 77:13). It is in sanctuary with Him where we get in touch with GOD and get to know His ways. It is here where our promises are fulfilled and all our difficulties are settled because we have become acquainted with Him in the hallowed place of worship and refuge.

There are many passages of Scripture that teach us how to get into the ways of GOD. We read in one of the psalms, "The humble He guides in justice, and the humble He teaches His way" (Psalm 25:9). Do you know what it is to be humble? It is to be unassuming, making no assertions of yourself, making no assertions of your old nature.

Do you know when we have our own way and our own desires they will keep us out of the will of GOD? But if we yield ourselves to the way of GOD, His Word declares, "Your ears shall hear a word behind you, saying, 'This is the way, walk in it,' whenever you turn to the right hand or whenever you turn to the left" (Isaiah 30:21). Furthermore, the LORD specifically promises His people that He will teach them His way. We read in Isaiah 2:3—

> *"Come, and let us go up to the mountain of the LORD, to the house of the GOD of Jacob; He will teach us His ways, and we shall walk in His*

> paths." For out of Zion shall go forth the law,
> and the word of the LORD from Jerusalem.

Oh, that we would understand GOD'S desire for us to learn of
His ways and to forsake those of our own.

2

Faith's Hindrance

*"You ran well. Who hindered you
from obeying the truth?" (Galatians 5:7)*

Before we can learn GOD's way, we need to consider our own ways. Where have our own ways brought us? Where will they bring us? The LORD said through Haggai to the children of Israel:

"Consider your ways! You have sown much, and bring in little; you eat, but do not have enough; you drink, but you are not filled with drink; you clothe yourselves, but no one is warm; and he who earns wages, earns wages to put into a bag with holes." (1:5-6)

> IT WON'T DO US ANY HARM TO LOOK OVER OUR PASTS AND SEE THE CHIEF HINDRANCES TO THE LIFE OF FAITH . . .

What have your labors brought in? Consider your ways. It won't do us any harm to look over our pasts and see the chief hindrances to the life of faith—our thoughts and our ways.

OUR THOUGHTS

The natural mind is constantly occupied with many things— thoughts and imaginations—which sometimes run like lightning. The devil is allowed to inject things into the mind; however, we are to blame for a lot of the machinery in our heads that is set in motion.

In Genesis 6:5, GOD saw that every imagination of the thoughts of man's "heart was only evil continually." This does not mean the thoughts of the unregenerate man are necessarily of murder and immorality, but it means that fallen man's thoughts are not GOD's thoughts. After the fall, the thought of GOD had departed out of the mind of man.

The great multitude of people today has no thought of GOD whatsoever. Their thoughts are evil and pertain to things natural, earthly, and selfish. Man's intellect has been terribly damaged by the devil in the fall. It is only the mighty power of GOD that can turn these thoughts in the right direction.

The newly regenerated man is awakened to a sense of a battle in the mind. When he begins to take a stand of faith, he recognizes there is a battle on. For example, he might receive prayer for a bad cold. Afterwards, he unthinkingly exclaims, "I have a bad cold." What is the matter? He evidently trusted sincerely in the LORD for healing, but thoughts have been permitted to operate in a contrary direction. These thoughts are a constant hindrance to the believer's life and stand of faith.

BELOVED, IF WE PRAY IN FAITH, WE SHOULD THINK IN FAITH.

Beloved, if we pray in faith, we should think in faith. But it is not in the natural mind to do so. We cannot even pray without our minds wandering. Per chance, thoughts of unbelief creep in and bind us. In the natural, we are helpless. But thank GOD for His precious HOLY SPIRIT who leads us and guides us into all truth.

Yes, GOD must come in and do something for us. Thank the LORD, salvation purchased on Calvary's cross is complete, embracing as it does the spirit, soul, and body. And its gracious provision includes the mind. Yet the only way to have believing minds is for the HOLY SPIRIT to take possession, and the first operation of the HOLY SPIRIT is decapitation—He takes off our heads.

Going back to our example of the newly regenerated man who received prayer for his bad cold, we may have found him, having taken such a stand of faith, questioning, "How is the LORD going to work this out?" He even may have wondered if it was really possible for GOD to intervene for him. Next, he may have questioned, "Is the LORD really willing to do this?" Such thoughts are permitted to darken the vision of the promise of GOD, but faith discerns clearly GOD's promise and stands resolutely upon it.

> . . . FAITH DISCERNS CLEARLY GOD'S PROMISE AND STANDS RESOLUTELY UPON IT.

Realize, too, there are unforgiving thoughts—thoughts of hatred and of fear—that have a tendency to bind and render man helpless. Fear reacts upon the body, inducing disease. This physiological fact is recognized by Christian Science. It teaches its votaries to practice good thoughts. "Don't think you are sick. Don't think you are a sinner. Think refined thoughts concerning yourself and other people," such religion teaches. It may be that this procedure accounts for some of the healings actually accomplished by the disciples of Mrs. Mary Baker Eddy!

Many physicians make it a practice when they come into a patient's room to be cheery and positive. They recognize this is the best medicine that can be given. They know the great power exercised by thoughts over the body.

This principle also holds true in the realm of the spiritual nature of man. As a man thinks, so is he (Proverbs 23:7).

Think evil thoughts, and the result will be evil actions.

THINK EVIL THOUGHTS, AND THE RESULT WILL BE EVIL ACTIONS.

We know, too, that bad habits originate in our thought life. Should a young Christian find difficulty breaking with an unclean habit, the safest thing to do, having renounced the habit as unclean, is to throw any of its paraphernalia in the fire. Burn up the bridges. Avoid places where others practice such habits, lest the old appetite should awaken.

We are slow to recognize the harmful effect that thoughts exercise, not only upon the body, but also upon the spirit. Thinking critically of our neighbor, for example, will work unfavorably upon our natures. It may cause us unnecessary grief and sorrow.

Yet another thing that can harm our spirits is unforgiveness. If we discover in ourselves an unforgiving spirit, we should confess and forsake it as we are admonished in Scripture, "'For if you forgive men their trespasses, your heavenly FATHER will also forgive you. But if you do not forgive men their trespasses, neither will your FATHER forgive your trespasses'" (Matthew 6:14-15). Please be careful, dear reader, lest unforgiveness bind both you and your offending brother.

And if thoughts of meanness regarding others arise, banish them from the mind as quickly as possible. Scripture admonishes us to cast "down arguments and every high thing that exalts itself against the knowledge of GOD, bringing every thought into captivity to the obedience of CHRIST" (2 Corinthians 10:5).

The Bible has a powerful influence on the mind. It is possible for a man to think he trusts the LORD when all the time unbelief is binding him. But "faith comes by hearing, and hearing by the word of GOD" (Romans 10:17); therefore, faith comes by the Word of GOD.

The blood of JESUS is also a powerful antidote against a disordered mind, for it so effectually purges the mind of evil that only holy thoughts can remain. We need to learn to appropriate the cleansing power of JESUS' blood.

Then there is the power of the SPIRIT which is manifested in the direction of control. He helps us control our thought life. As the Scripture says, "When the enemy comes in like a flood, the SPIRIT OF THE LORD will lift up a standard against him" (Isaiah 59:19).

Someone has said, "We cannot hinder the birds from flying over our heads, but we can hinder them from making their nests in our hair." If you harbor a wrong thought, it will get into your heart, and the first thing you know, it influences your actions

> **WE HAVE POWER TO REFUSE THE WRONG THOUGHT.**

and breaks down your spirit. We have power to refuse the wrong thought. Glory to JESUS for His victory!

OUR WAYS

Ways and habits proceed from thoughts. When we come to the LORD, we have habits which already have been formed. These habits originate in the affections, appetites, and desires. They may even dwell in the physical being as well as in the soul.

We do certain things instinctively. Many of these actions obstruct the way of GOD, for they are contrary to the mind of GOD. When the HOLY SPIRIT comes in, it is to take up His abode. Perhaps this explains why some people shake violently under the operation of the SPIRIT—because of the conflict which is taking place between Him and their flesh.

Other conflicts arise in our lives because of different kinds of habits which are injurious to growth in grace, for example—overeating, late rising, perpetual lateness, habitual slackness in prayer, neglect of systematic devotional Bible study. One reason people attend Bible school is to form right habits of study, of prayer, and of reading the Scriptures. If one leaves Bible school with habits unformed upon the lines I have indicated, we are disappointed, and he will have missed the purpose for which the Bible school was established.

When he gets out into ministry, there will be demands for service made upon him, and he may discover he is unequal to these demands, causing him to give his time to secondary things. Beloved, we all should practice now the things that will be best for us so as not to frustrate the work of ministry or the work of GOD in our lives.

> BELOVED, WE ALL SHOULD PRACTICE NOW THE THINGS THAT WILL BE BEST FOR US SO AS NOT TO FRUSTRATE THE WORK OF MINISTRY OR THE WORK OF GOD IN OUR LIVES.

We must be ever mindful that our natural ways block our progress heavenwards, thus frustrating us and possibly inducing depression in us. We little realize how unformed habits frustrate faith and trust in the LORD. The LORD wants us to forsake our ways and abandon ourselves to His.

LEARNING HIS WAY

Let's look at examples of those who forsook their own ways and learned the ways of GOD. Consider again the Apostle Paul when the LORD spoke to him about going up to Rome. In the natural, one might have thought Paul would have had a comfortable ride in a chariot on his journey to Rome, but Paul was obliged to travel as a prisoner in that sailing vessel. Yet in that vessel, they had to pull up all the anchors, hoist the main sail, and let the boat drive right in the storm. Again, this is what GOD calls us to do—let go of everything that would hold us, abandon ourselves to Him, take our hands off, believe that He is at the helm, and learn to go on in the will of GOD! GOD'S way is not the easy way of sailing; it's exactly the opposite.

Naaman, captain of the host of the King of Syria, found this out. He said, "'Indeed, I said to myself, "He [the prophet Elisha] will surely come out to me, and stand and call on the name of the LORD his GOD, and wave his hand over the place, and heal the leprosy"'" (2 Kings 5:11). To go down and dip seven times in Jordan as Naaman was bid touched the pride of this haughty man. He had to forsake his ideas of how it was he should be healed so that he could receive his healing.

> [NAAMAN] HAD TO FORSAKE HIS IDEAS OF HOW IT WAS HE SHOULD BE HEALED SO THAT HE COULD RECEIVE HIS HEALING.

And let us not forget Peter, whose ways—on more than one occasion—cut against those of His Master. When, for instance, Peter stepped out of the boat to go to JESUS, he did not step out on water. He stepped out on JESUS' word. Peter's first steps were in faith, and he could have kept walking by faith, but his eyes saw a big wave, as it were. Since he had always lived on the plane of sight and feeling, that was his way, he went down at the sight of the wave.

The devil knows that by nature we live in the sense realm, so he lets waves roll up in front of us whenever we step out on the Word of GOD to step into GOD'S ways. But which are we to believe, our senses that have misled us time and time again or the Word of GOD which does not lie?

Think, too, of what Martha said to JESUS when He came to the grave of Lazarus. "'LORD, if You had been here, my brother would not have died. But even now I know that whatever You ask of GOD, GOD will give You'" (John 11:21-22). "Even now!" Most of our hymns are hymns of the past or the future. These furnish a good background and a good outlook, but I can live with a good background and a good outlook and never get very far. I need something *right now* in my present experience.

HOW OFTEN THE SAVING, HEALING, AND MIRACLE-WORKING POWER OF CHRIST HAS BEEN RESTRICTED . . . BY MEN'S LACK OF FAITH.

JESUS began to work upon Martha's expression of faith. I believe He recognized the tense of her faith —"Even now." Do you know our use of tenses affects our faith? How often the saving, healing, and miracle-working power of CHRIST has been restricted to Bible times by men's lack of faith. And many, who believe it is for the present day, limit the LORD by their faithless expressions of, "I know He can heal me when He gets ready." But should we not believe His Word? Can we not say with Martha, "Even now," and see GOD work for us in the present, for GOD'S time is now?

Martha said, "'But even now I know that whatever You ask of GOD, GOD will give You'" (John 11:22).

JESUS responded, "'Your brother will rise again'" (23).

"'I know that he will rise again in the resurrection at the last day,'" affirmed Martha (24).

Then JESUS said to her, "'I am the resurrection and the life. He who believes in Me, though he may die, he shall live. And whoever lives and believes in Me shall never die. Do you believe this?'" (25-26).

Martha's reply to this moved beyond her "even now" statement of faith. Hers was a confession much like that of Peter's when JESUS asked him, "'But who do you say that I am?'" (Matthew 16:15-16). Martha said, "'Yes, LORD, I believe that You are the CHRIST, the SON OF GOD, who is to come into the world'" (John 11:27).

With this, Martha acknowledged her letting go of how she thought JESUS should have addressed the issue of her brother's sickness and later demise. Here, she abandoned her thoughts and ways and embraced the way of THE RESUR-RECTION AND THE LIFE. She, like Peter before her, came to the place of understanding just who JESUS was, and I believe like Peter she came to understand this by the revelation of the FATHER through the work of the HOLY SPIRIT (Matthew 16:17).

THE HOLY SPIRIT'S WORK

Looking back at the story of Peter in the boat, we read that JESUS said, "'Come,'" to him, thus prompting him to step out into the water (Matthew 14:29). JESUS says to the world today, "Come." His SPIRIT says to us, "Come." Be encouraged, dear reader, there are not enough devils to hinder any individual who will come to GOD in faith. JESUS said, "'The one who comes to Me I will by no means cast out'" (John 6:37).

Knowing your thoughts and your ways are contrary to GOD's, do you want to get rid of your old man, of your old ways? Paul says in Romans 6:6, "Our old man was crucified with Him." There is indeed power in Calvary, but is that all you are to do is recognize the fact? No! Paul says, "Likewise you also, reckon yourselves to be dead indeed to sin, but alive to GOD in CHRIST JESUS our LORD" (Romans 6:11). That is where faith comes in. It makes the basis for the HOLY SPIRIT to work.

> **THAT IS WHERE FAITH COMES IN. IT MAKES THE BASIS FOR THE HOLY SPIRIT TO WORK.**

Go a few verses further, and he says, "Present yourselves to GOD" (13). There are people who strongly and firmly believe in the fundamentals of the atonement, but they are not finding the SPIRIT OF GOD. Their ideas are merely theoretical for they have yet to offer themselves—to present their bodies—as living sacrifices (Romans 12:1).

If the SPIRIT OF THE LORD accomplishes anything through us, it will be because He has moved us out of our natural ways and because we have learned not to rely on that which is earthly, human, and ordinary. Instead, it will be because we have learned to have faith in the GOD who is invisible.

In 2 Samuel 22:34, we read, "'He makes my feet like the feet of deer, and sets me on my high places.'" If we walk GOD'S way, He must make our feet small, so we can walk the narrow way and walk up the rugged rocks of going higher with Him. It's the path of trial. It's the good old rugged way of the cross.

Man's nature—like that of Paul, Naaman, Peter, and Martha—always looks for an easy path and an easy way. That

> **MAN'S NATURE ALWAYS LOOKS FOR AN EASY PATH AND AN EASY WAY.**

is the human way. That's the way of the world. As we choose the way of the cross, however, the LORD will work through His providences and shape our destinies by the SPIRIT's power, cleansing us of our way and bringing us into His way. Through His shed blood, we can enter into His way in faith.

3

THROUGH THE BLOOD IS . . .
Faith's Approach

> *"Therefore, brethren, having boldness to enter the Holiest by the blood of JESUS, by a new and living way which He consecrated for us, through the veil, that is, His flesh, and having a High Priest over the house of GOD, let us draw near with a true heart in full assurance of faith, having our hearts sprinkled from an evil conscience and our bodies washed with pure water." (Hebrews 10:19-22)*

The above Scripture tells us how we can be cleansed from our way and enter the way to GOD. It is through the Holiest or Holy of Holies—where GOD always was present in the Jewish tabernacle. The ark was there; on the ark was the Mercy Seat, and on the Mercy Seat was the blood. It was the only meeting place of GOD and man. In fact, there is no other place of meeting GOD today but at the Mercy Seat.

> . . . THERE IS NO OTHER PLACE OF MEETING GOD TODAY BUT AT THE MERCY SEAT.

Romans 3:24-25 points us to a new covenant version of the Jewish tabernacle's place of meeting. It reads, "Being justified freely by His grace through the redemption that is in CHRIST JESUS, whom GOD set forth as a propitiation by His blood, through faith, to demonstrate His righteousness." The word "propitiation" is translated from the Greek word, *hilasterion*, which means Mercy Seat.

From this, we can declare JESUS is our Mercy Seat!

THE NEW AND LIVING WAY

JESUS did not enter into the earthly tabernacle once every year with the blood of sheep and goats as did the Hebrew High Priest, for we read, "But this Man, after He had offered one sacrifice for sins forever, sat down at the right hand of GOD" (Hebrews 10:12). He entered into the heavenly tabernacle once with His own blood to offer for our eternal redemption. And by this one offering, "He has perfected forever those who are being sanctified" (Hebrews 10:14).

All our salvation from our ways, our sin, and our sickness and all the impartations of life, grace, and faith depend upon our meeting GOD. Our spiritual advancement also depends on a constant, actual touch from GOD. Therefore, we see the importance of this Scripture that we are to enter with boldness this new and living way, approaching the throne of grace in faith.

But let us look back again to the wilderness wanderings of the children of Israel. There were always the morning and evening sacrifices and with them the shedding of blood. The sacrifices were ever before them. We should always keep the vision of Calvary before us and the shedding of our SAVIOR's precious blood. This is the only source and basis for spiritual development and growth. The vision of Calvary gives us a basis for faith. Nothing will I ever receive from GOD through natural struggle or self-effort but on the basis of faith in the blood.

> NOTHING WILL I EVER RECEIVE FROM GOD THROUGH NATURAL STRUGGLE OR SELF-EFFORT BUT ON THE BASIS OF FAITH IN THE BLOOD.

So let us draw near with a true heart, a heart that is honest to GOD and fully surrendered to Him—a heart that truly abandons itself to Him and to the authority and power of the blood. Our hearts must choose the new and living way and desire the indwelling and lordship of JESUS. Doubtless there are hidden depths of sin in our flesh of which we are not yet conscious. Under the searching light of the HOLY SPIRIT, revelation is made of these inherent states. For them also is propitiation made in the shed blood. Then, as we yield to GOD, the blood can cleanse them all away.

There must be also a full assurance of faith. We should take time to meditate upon what is done for us in this marvelous sacrifice. As we do this, faith will spring up. It will bring forth that for which our hearts are longing.

Additionally, our hearts must be sprinkled from an evil conscience. No one ever gets anything from GOD when his heart is under condemnation. Romans 8:1 tells us, "There is therefore now no condemnation to those who are in CHRIST JESUS, who do not walk according to the flesh, but according to the SPIRIT." However, if you are smitten with a guilty conscience because of an inward sinful way, let it cause you to flee to Calvary for a fresh cleansing by the blood. As you flee, the guilt all goes away.

> NO ONE EVER GETS ANYTHING FROM GOD WHEN HIS HEART IS UNDER CONDEMNATION.

Many are conscious in these days that GOD is taking issue with them because of their lack of spiritual growth. They have a sense of the coming of awful judgments upon the world as the Day of the LORD draws near. The blood speaks for us today, not because it was shed upon the earth, but it speaks in heaven as JESUS carried His blood therein with Him. Therefore, in the judgment scenes that are coming, GOD says, ""When I see the blood, I will pass over you""" (Exodus 12:13).

We can look back at a time before the first Passover, the time Noah built the ark. The ark was a place of safety from the judgments of that day. JESUS is the Ark of Safety for His people in the last judgment hour of these last days. The Scripture says this ark was daubed with pitch to keep the waters of judgment out. In the margin of the King James Version, the word, "pitch," is called "atonement." The only protection in the hour of judgment is the application of the blood of atonement. The only entry to GOD's way is through faith in the efficacious blood of CHRIST.

> **THE ONLY ENTRY TO GOD'S WAY IS THROUGH FAITH IN THE EFFICACIOUS BLOOD OF CHRIST.**

SEEING THE WAY

I am so glad that JESUS said, "'I am the way'" (John 14:6). Get your eyes upon JESUS. Let Him fill your vision for He will lead you out of your old ways, out of the natural into the supernatural. We have a promise in these last days of the greatest measure and quality of the supernatural being manifest that the world has ever known. If you and I don't get into His ways, it is because we are unwilling to let go. Let go, and let the LORD have His way.

GOD always has worked on this principle of faith, and He always will. We read in Romans 1:16-17,

> *For I am not ashamed of the gospel of CHRIST, for it is the power of GOD to salvation for everyone who believes, for the Jew first and also for the Greek. For in it the righteousness of GOD is*

> *revealed from faith to faith; as it is written,
> "The just shall live by faith."*

The righteousness of GOD is revealed from faith to faith or by faith to faith. In other words, it is a by-faith-righteousness. It is neither a worked-up-righteousness nor a righteousness of any human origin, but it is the righteousness of GOD that comes to us on the basis of faith. So it is with everything we receive from GOD.

One of the most outstanding difficulties that inhibits us from coming into the way of faith is that we have learned all of our lives to walk, to do, to know, and to under-

> . . . IT IS THE
> RIGHTEOUSNESS OF
> GOD THAT COMES TO
> US ON THE BASIS
> OF FAITH.

stand by our natural senses of sight, hearing, and feeling. As a result, men live their lives in sense knowledge. All our thinking has been on that plane, but it will never bring us to GOD.

Man by wisdom can never know GOD, and yet how people (even saved people) try to understand GOD and the things of GOD through their natural senses. But spiritual things never can be received on this plane. *Oh, GOD, help us to see it with our spiritual eyes that the only way we will ever come to an understanding of You and Your ways is by revelation.*

Truth that is revealed by GOD cannot be understood naturally. The schools of higher learning do not prepare one to understand it. But when we receive a touch of GOD and faith touches the Word of GOD, JESUS is revealed in our hearts and lives. Then supposition ends for we know we have eternal life. We know JESUS is our SAVIOR, and we know He is our Healer because there has entered into the heart life revealed truth from the Word of GOD.

We should understand the difference between these two types of knowledge and the way they are obtained so that we might shun our natural understanding and with open hearts say to the LORD, "I believe Your Word." For we read, "The entrance of Your words gives light; it gives understanding to the simple" (Psalm 119:130).

Through faith, Hebrews 11:3 tells us that the worlds were framed by the Word of GOD. GOD's Word comes forth by the avenue of faith, for our GOD is a faith GOD. All that GOD has done has been done on the basis of faith in His Word. As I've said before, He spoke, and it was. That is the way He works, not only in creation but in everything. The Word of GOD has power to bring to pass what He says.

> GOD'S WORD COMES FORTH BY THE AVENUE OF FAITH, FOR OUR GOD IS A FAITH GOD. ALL THAT GOD HAS DONE HAS BEEN DONE ON THE BASIS OF FAITH IN HIS WORD.

ENTERING THE WAY

How do we obtain salvation? How do we obtain healing? How do we obtain righteousness? By faith in what GOD says! By faith in the efficacy of His blood! Praise the LORD!

My own personal experience is that the vision of Calvary and the resurrection will generate faith. If you have not the vision, that is what you need. In all these years of GOD's dealings with me, when I have come up to some fresh place and was right on its threshold, GOD always has dealt with me to see whether it was found in Calvary or not. When I questioned Divine healing and saw it in Calvary, I was satisfied. It is the same with the baptism of the SPIRIT, the outpourings, and victory over the world, the flesh, and the devil—all because JESUS won them on the cross.

Just because we see all that is in the atonement, however, does not mean we have it. It is up to us to enter into, possess, and count upon all that was purchased for us by the blood of CHRIST. Once we approach GOD's ways through faith in the blood, we must allow the HOLY SPIRIT to make real our position in CHRIST so we may stand complete in Him.

> IT IS UP TO US TO ENTER INTO, POSSESS, AND COUNT UPON ALL THAT WAS PURCHASED FOR US BY THE BLOOD OF CHRIST.

4

Faith's Position

"For if the blood of bulls and goats and the ashes of a heifer,
sprinkling the unclean, sanctifies for the purifying of the flesh,
how much more shall the blood of CHRIST, who through the
eternal SPIRIT offered Himself without spot to GOD, cleanse
your conscience from dead works to serve the living GOD?"
(Hebrews 9:13-14)

As we see in GOD's Word, JESUS CHRIST was not a victim. He was wholly offered up to the will of GOD as a voluntary offering to make atonement for the sins of man. His was an offering without blemish and by fire. The fire speaks of the suffering of the cross which He endured to atone for our sins. He laid down His life for us; no man or other being took it from Him.

> JESUS WAS WHOLLY OFFERED UP TO THE WILL OF GOD AS A VOLUNTARY OFFERING.

In the Old Testament, we are given types and shadows alluding to JESUS' sacrifice. Specifically, we see a type in the red heifer mentioned in Hebrews 9 and in Numbers 19.

THE TYPE

This red heifer mentioned in Hebrews 9:13 is a type of CHRIST, representing purification and separation unto GOD. GOD said it is a statute (or memorial) forever, typifying the eternal sacrifice of JESUS CHRIST for sin (Numbers 19:10).

According to the instructions given in Numbers 19, the heifer was to be burned by one man, and its ashes were to be gathered by another. They were then laid without the camp in a clean place (8-9).

As we read of the sacrifice of the red heifer, the question arises, "Why red?" Red, of course, speaks of sacrifice, of blood. Hebrews 9:22, tell us that "without shedding of blood there is no remission" of sin. Blood represents the life of the flesh—"'"For the life of the flesh is in the blood, and I have given it to you upon the altar to make atonement for your souls; for it is the blood that makes atonement for the soul"'" (Leviticus 17:11).

JESUS Himself shed His blood upon Calvary to atone for the sins of His people as I have said already. His blood was shed for you and for me, and not for Himself. He had no sin. The sin is in the blood, in the flesh, but JESUS' blood was pure. He was born as the SON OF GOD. When His blood flowed out, it did not take His life. That is not what took the life of JESUS. He gave up His spirit after the blood had flowed from His body. He dismissed His spirit. He had power to lay down His life and power to take it up again. This was not so with the red heifer. But she was only a type or shadow of what was to come. She was to be sacrificed outside the camp and her whole carcass burned.

THE WHOLE BURNT OFFERING

There was a difference in sacrifices in the Old Testament. Some of the animals were only sacrificed in part, and the rest of the carcass was given to the priests for their food. But that was not the case with the whole burnt offering.

The whole burnt offering speaks of JESUS' giving His all to

the LORD—without reservation. He gave His reputation, His heavenly home in glory. He gave all that He had, His very life. He sacrificed His fellowship with GOD the FATHER and cried on the cross, "'My GOD, My GOD, why have You forsaken Me?'" (Mark 15:34). He became the laughingstock of the drunkards. He suffered in His

> THE WHOLE BURNT OFFERING SPEAKS OF JESUS' GIVING HIS ALL TO THE LORD— WITHOUT RESERVATION.

flesh and spirit life. He gave all, hallelujah, as a whole burnt offering to the FATHER in the will of GOD that His sacrifice might be complete and might fully satisfy a broken law of GOD and satisfy the holiness and righteous standards of GOD!

The completeness of that sacrifice only GOD can ever reveal to us. What it meant to bring a complete satisfaction for the broken laws of GOD is more than I can express. Praise the LORD forever! And He did it in my stead. It was my place to suffer for my sin and my shame, but He took my place and gave me His place instead. He gave me, the same as any believer in faith, a position before GOD as though I had never sinned. He put me in a position before GOD as righteous as He is righteous, as holy as He is holy. That is my standing before GOD because my standing before GOD is in JESUS. GOD sees me through JESUS. He sees me through His precious blood, declaring me, "Not guilty!" This is true justification for every believer.

> HE GAVE ME, THE SAME AS ANY BELIEVER IN FAITH, A POSITION BEFORE GOD AS THOUGH I HAD NEVER SINNED.

THE ASH HEAP

So, the sin question was settled.
Now, there was a special significance in the ashes here. They

seem just ashes—the ashes of a heifer. These ashes were gathered and carried out. Notice they were placed in a clean place. And they were used with water and hyssop. This hyssop was dipped in the water and ashes and then sprinkled on the unclean and the entire tabernacle and its furniture.

What did the sprinkling speak of? Cleansing and purification. The ashes spoke of a sacrifice complete. The water speaks of the HOLY SPIRIT. It is the ashes of the sacrifice of the whole burnt HOLY SPIRIT. The HOLY SPIRIT applies the ashes of the whole burnt offering for purification. So it is the work of the sacrifice of Calvary applied by the HOLY SPIRIT that purifies. Praise the LORD for this complete redemption! It was mainly for GOD'S people in purification from daily sins, not so much the sins of the past but for the daily mistakes. Thank GOD, the sacrifice of JESUS speaks for us every day. "And if anyone sins," John wrote, "we have an Advocate with the FATHER, JESUS CHRIST the righteous" (1 John 2:1).

> THANK GOD, THE SACRIFICE OF JESUS SPEAKS FOR US EVERY DAY.

Let's turn to another place in Scripture that speaks of the ash heap. In the book of Job, we find Job sitting among the ashes. He sat among the ashes—"And he took for himself a potsherd with which to scrape himself while he sat in the midst of the ashes" (Job 2:8).

There are a good many ash heaps that Job could have sat down on while in his dilemma. Lots of ash heaps we meet today—ash heaps of discouragement, of self-pity, of borrowed troubles. But you sit down on those ashes, and you don't get anywhere spiritually. I believe Job sat down on the right ash heap—an ash heap of hope. Job could have said, "Now, this ash heap speaks of my redemption, my cleansing." We read, however, that he said, "'And after my skin is destroyed, this I know, that in my flesh I shall see GOD'" (Job 19:26).

Yes, we have a lot of ash heaps today. These are discouraging days. Beloved, the more we grumble and complain the worse we get. But there is one ash heap to be upon that brings victory, comfort, *and* faith. Hallelujah! Come out of the condition you are in. GOD'S hand is upon you, and He will see you through. You can shout with Job, "'Though He slay me, yet will I trust Him'" (13:15).

I don't suppose any of us will ever be tested any more than Job was, and through the testing, purification came evidently because Job was on the right ash heap. For we find afterward he mentioned, "'I have heard of You by the hearing of the ear, but now my eye sees You. Therefore I abhor myself, and repent in dust and ashes'" (42:5-6).

Apparently, Job couldn't speak this way before. He came to the end of himself, and repented in sackcloth and ashes. And what was the result? Out of that condition, Job came into a position of faith and victory and hope—a glo-

> . . . JOB CAME INTO A POSITION OF FAITH AND VICTORY AND HOPE— A GLORIOUS RESTORATION . . .

rious restoration—so that GOD brought back to him twice as much wealth as he had before.

The last end of Job was greater than that of the first. That speaks of us in our day. We receive the best of the wine at the end of the feast. Joel said:

> *"So I will restore to you the years that the swarming locust has eaten, the crawling locust, the consuming locust, and the chewing locust, My great army which I sent among you. You shall*

eat in plenty and be satisfied, and praise the name of the LORD your GOD, who has dealt wondrously with you; and My people shall never be put to shame." (2:25-26)

Yes, when we see the last end of Job, we begin to understand God's intended end. The Scripture says, "You have heard of the perseverance of Job and seen the end intended by the LORD" (James 5:11). Where was Job's perseverance manifest? In the scraping of his boils? No! His perseverance in still sitting on the ash heap of expectation, of anticipation, and of victory. His wife said, "'Curse GOD and die!'" (Job 2:9). And Job could have done it. He saw a way of blessing, of life, of victory, of hope, and of cleansing. He entered that way and stayed in place until the work was complete.

GOD is after us these days. He is after His people, purifying, separating—separating and purifying unto Himself. Where are we? Are we sitting on the right ash heap? Are we staying there?

But let's read the words of James again: "You have heard of the perseverance of Job and seen the end intended by the LORD—that the LORD is very compassionate and merciful." What was the intended end of the LORD? It was to show Job His great compassion and mercy. When GOD takes care of your case and mine as He took charge of Job's case, He will come to the scene in His time. Stand upon the sacrifice of Calvary, hold to the sprinkling blood, to the cleansing of the blood of JESUS CHRIST. Let the SPIRIT OF

STAND UPON THE SACRIFICE OF CALVARY, HOLD TO THE SPRINKLING BLOOD, TO THE CLEANSING OF THE BLOOD OF JESUS CHRIST.

GOD work it out within us all its purifying power, if it takes years and years and years. You will see the intended end of the LORD. GOD always begins where we end. When we get through, GOD undertakes. That's the end of the LORD. That was the end Job saw, and the deliverance came.

Don't you see? It is the way of faith. It is the stand in faith of the sacrifice that was once made. It is the faith that abides, that counts on JESUS—counts on Him yesterday, today, and always. That faith that counts on Him for what He has done on Calvary. He will do a new and fresh work for us today and will also do something fresh for us tomorrow. He will go on to a perfect work.

This way of faith is an outstanding way. It is the way of victory. Praise GOD! Let us rejoice in the plan of redemption. Allow the cross to have its perfect work in our lives. Allow it to cleanse and purify us until the dross is all burned away and JESUS stands supreme in our lives. Here

THIS WAY OF FAITH IS AN OUTSTANDING WAY.

we're justified. Here faith's position is realized. And here we stand firmly on faith's foundation.

5

CHvRIST IS . . .

Faith's Foundation

"For no other foundation can anyone lay than that which is laid, which is JESUS CHRIST." (1 Corinthians 3:11)

The cross interprets the character of GOD. Man would never have known the love of GOD had not JESUS given His life as a ransom. Neither would the holy and righteous character of GOD be made manifest without the cross of Calvary.

> **THE CROSS INTERPRETS THE CHARACTER OF GOD.**

The law, which is a revelation of the righteousness of GOD, was broken by sinful man. In exacting its power upon JESUS as the sinner's Substitute, the righteous character of GOD was vindicated and upheld. As Romans 3:24 and 26 reads:

> *Being justified freely by His grace through the redemption that is in CHRIST JESUS . . . to demonstrate at the present time His righteousness, that He might be just and the justifier of the one who has faith in JESUS.*

What is needed today is clear revelation of Calvary both to sinner and saint. Today, both the love and holiness of GOD are considered as merely human things because of a lack of vision of Calvary, yet one only sees these things by Divine revelation.

If the justice of GOD in venting its wrath upon the Substi-

tute for the sinner took the life of the SON OF GOD (not merely a man), what must His justice be on those who reject Him?
Pilate said, "'What then shall I do with JESUS who is called the
CHRIST?'" (Matthew 27:22). Their answer was to send JESUS to
the cross.

> **BUT CHRIST'S WORK
> ON THE CROSS IS THE
> VERY BASIS FOR FAITH
> AND BLESSING!
> IT IS THE FOUNDATION
> OF OUR FAITH IN HIM.**

But CHRIST'S work on the cross
is the very basis for faith and blessing! It is the foundation of our faith
in Him.

REDEMPTION

Recently, my attention was drawn
to Psalm 96, which naturally falls
into four parts. The first three verses call us to "Declare His
glory among the nations, His wonders among all peoples" (3).
The next three verses contrast our JEHOVAH with the gods of
the heathen. The next three are a call to worship Him in "the
beauty of holiness." And the last four verses make reference to
the release of nature and humanity from the curse in GOD'S
final glorious triumph.

Let us take special note of verse 10 in this psalm: "Say
among the nations, 'The LORD reigns.'" An early Greek man-
uscript reads a little differently—"Say among the heathen that
the LORD reigneth from the tree."

Justin Martyr, one of the early church fathers, said the
phrase, "from the tree," had been deleted by the Jews to cover
the obvious reference to CHRIST. But, thank GOD, it is clearly
set forth in the New Testament: JEHOVAH reigns from the tree.
The name JESUS means JEHOVAH our SAVIOR, and He could
only save us by hanging on a tree—but there He reigns!

Think again of JESUS' being questioned before Pilate. We
read that Pilate marveled greatly and that he found no fault in

JESUS. But the people cried, "Away with Him! Crucify Him!" Though Pilate requested Him to do so, JESUS spoke not a word of defense for He came into this world to reign from the tree. In His spirit, there was a majestic humility and serenity even though He knew what was soon to take place. He was a captive of Rome on trial, yet in His spirit He was Victor!

One often hears, "GOD is too loving to send a man to hell," or "Hell is not eternal." Listen, if the love of GOD was so infinite that it brought the SON OF GOD to make the ultimate sacrifice of separation from GOD and led Him to suffer the awful agonies of Calvary, what is the measure of that love?

After Pilate released JESUS to the Jews, the Roman soldiers took charge of Him, stripped Him, pressed a crown of thorns on His head, placed a reed in His hand, and mockingly said, "Hail, King of the Jews!" Purple is a type of royalty, and a crown always speaks of the same. JESUS never was and never will be more of a king than He was that day.

Many have thought that JESUS died as a victim of foul play by an angry mob. As I have said before, He died not as a victim; He offered up His life as a Victor.

From His head, His side, His hands, and His feet, blood flowed. Every drop that struck the ground

> [JESUS] DIED NOT AS A VICTIM; HE OFFERED UP HIS LIFE AS A VICTOR.

said, "Redemption, redemption, redemption!" He wore the crown of thorns, a part of the curse, as He reigned from the tree. The greatest victory of all time took place that day. The curse was there lifted. Deliverance came for all humanity, and satan received his death blow!

John in Revelation 5 saw a book written inside and out and sealed with seven seals. This is the book of redemption. In Jewish economy, when one lost his property and had sold himself into slavery to pay his debts, the whole record was written in a book. The book was then sealed with seven seals and put in the temple. The one who was in servitude because of his debt was given a book also, but it was left open so he could read it. If at least a kinsman was found able to pay the debt, he could have the book and break the seals, releasing this man and his family from servitude.

No wonder John wept when he saw this book and saw that no man in heaven or on earth was worthy to break the seals. Then one of the elders came and said, "'Do not weep. Behold, the Lion of the tribe of Judah, the Root of David, has prevailed to open the scroll and to loose its seven seals'" (Revelation 5:5). But when he looked he saw a lamb, not a lion. This word, "lamb," means a wee lamb, a bleeding lambkin as though it had been slain.

Here is manifested the triumphant weakness of GOD. "And as a sheep before its shearers is silent, so He opened not His mouth" (Isaiah 53:7). Our salvation is based on the sacrifice of a bleeding LAMB, and all that we have received or will receive from GOD comes through faith in Him.

> ... SALVATION IS BASED ON THE SACRIFICE OF A BLEEDING LAMB, AND ALL THAT WE HAVE RECEIVED OR WILL RECEIVE FROM GOD COMES THROUGH FAITH IN HIM.

But at Calvary, we see two aspects to this work: that which JESUS did *for* us and that which He did *to* us or *in* us. At Calvary, He made room in our hearts for His indwelling and delivered us not only from sin but from self and self-seeking.

THE INDWELLING PRESENCE

The great purpose of GOD in this generation is not only to

save people from sin and hell and to heal bodies—glorious as all this is—but it is to bring us back to Himself and indwell us in His fullness.

We like the psalmist can say, "I shall be satisfied when I awake in Your likeness" (17:15). But before we receive the JESUS of resurrection life in His fullness, we must know the JESUS of the cross and know that emptiness, humility, and separation from all that is not GOD-like. The Bride of CHRIST must have a lambkin spirit; the LAMB is preparing such a Bride.

Only in the measure that CHRIST reigns in our lives will His triumph be manifested in our ministry. We sometimes think that if we had talents, training, or what others have we could accomplish much for the Master. But the only way to effective service is through a laid down life. Paul learned this for he said, "For when I am weak, then I am strong" (2 Corinthians 12:10).

> OURS IS AN APPOINT-
> MENT UNTO DEATH—
> A DEATH TO ALL THE
> PAST, A DEATH TO ALL
> SELF-SUFFICIENCY, A
> DEATH TO ALL ABILITY
> —AND A COMING ALIVE
> TO FAITH IN GOD AND
> EXPERIENCING THE
> PRESENCE OF GOD . . .

An hour of stripping has come upon you and upon us all. Ours is an appointment unto death—a death to all the past, a death to all self-sufficiency, a death to all ability—and a coming alive to faith in GOD and experiencing the Presence of GOD within.

The Apostle Paul told Timothy:

> *For if we died with Him, we shall also live with Him. If we endure, we shall also reign with Him. If we deny Him, He also will deny us. If we are faithless, He remains faithful; He can-*

not deny Himself. (2 Timothy 2:11-13)

No, dear reader, CHRIST cannot deny Himself. He is true, and He is faithful. He is faith's foundation. And CHRIST, our sure foundation, "stands, having this seal: 'The LORD knows those who are His'" (2 Timothy 2:19). And He loves those who are His.

6

Faith's Motivation

"For in CHRIST JESUS *neither circumcision nor uncircumcision avails anything, but faith working through love."*
(Galatians 5:6)

We read in Romans 10:17, "So then faith comes by hearing, and hearing by the word of GOD." This does not mean that we only hear the written Word, but that we hear the spoken Word as well—the voice of GOD speaking definitely to our individual hearts. When GOD speaks to us and brings a conviction, our hearts open to the Word, and we step out into a new place in the LORD.

The blind beggar in the tenth chapter of Mark took such a step. According to the story, he threw aside his garments and went to JESUS (50). Evidently, the old garments of Bartimaeus meant nothing to him if he could receive his sight; he showed an attitude of faith and expectation.

Bartimaeus, as we read, cried first, "'JESUS, SON OF DAVID, have mercy on me!'" (47).

> . . . THE LORD IS SAYING TO US, "WHAT DO YOU WANT ME TO DO FOR YOU?"

But when the LORD turned to him with the question, "'What do you want Me to do for you?'" Bartimaeus was very definite in his request.

He said, "'Rabboni, that I may receive my sight'" (51).

It didn't take Bartimaeus any length of time to tell JESUS what he was seeking! Doubtless the LORD is saying to us, "What do you want Me to do for you?" JESUS recognizes a definite request.

Our LORD's reply to the blind man was, "'Go your way; your faith has made you well'" (52). And immediately Bartimaeus received his sight.

This is a simple little story, a sample of those that fill the New Testament, but it expresses a great truth: Be definite in your request to GOD. Remember when you wanted salvation, you were definite in your request, and you were saved. How about when you wanted healing, you were specific in expressing your need, and you were healed. Be definite in expressing your need, for real faith works on definite requests.

> . . . REAL FAITH WORKS ON DEFINITE REQUESTS . . . GENUINE FAITH WORKS ON THE BASIS OF LOVE.

OUR BASIS FOR FAITH

I wonder if we realize today how much real faith is dependent upon the love of GOD. We read at the opening of this chapter, "For in CHRIST JESUS neither circumcision nor uncircumcision avails anything, but faith working through love" (Galatians 5:6). When we come to the LORD for anything, do we think of Him as a hard taskmaster, and is there a fear in our spirits? Sometimes, fear will stir our hearts—fear of judgment, fear of failure, or fear of disappointment—and, in a way, it may be of some help to faith, but genuine faith works on the basis of love. Perhaps this is what drew Bartimaeus to cry out in faith to JESUS. Love is faith's complete motivation.

What basis do you have to expect anything from GOD? If you need healing, if you need heart cleansing, if you need a victory in your life, what basis have you to expect it? The basis is Calvary, and Calvary is the manifestation of GOD'S love.

Indeed we need today a heart revelation of the love of GOD. With that heart revelation will come an impartation to our lives, a flame and passion which will grip us until it carries us out of ourselves, until it makes us love the LORD so that we would rather abide in His Presence than do anything else in the world. Out of the fullness of that heart of love, then, will spring faith, a faith for the seeming impossible.

> OUT OF THE FULLNESS OF THAT HEART OF LOVE, THEN, WILL SPRING FAITH, A FAITH FOR THE SEEMING IMPOSSIBLE.

This should challenge us to stir up our faith. Timothy was in a hard place and feeling pretty badly about it, but Paul instructed him to stir up the gift within him. He said,

> *I call to remembrance the genuine faith that is in you, which dwelt first in your grandmother Lois and your mother Eunice, and I am persuaded is in you also. Therefore I remind you to stir up the gift of GOD which is in you through the laying on of my hands. For GOD has not given us a spirit of fear, but of power and of love and of a sound mind. (2 Timothy 1:5-7)*

It is very easy to just let up or become negligent and thus fail to press on spiritually. But Paul said Timothy had "genuine faith," and he said, "stir up," this gift of faith.

Our faith needs to be stirred in these days—read the Bible, pray, visit the saints and talk with them of the LORD's faithfulness, get into meetings, and stir up your faith. Do anything to bring your faith up, for we do not want to lose out, get lukewarm, or become Laodicean in our spirits in this hour.

We have something in us that will cut the shoreline—that will overcome opposition. May we let GOD move within us, remembering He has not given us a spirit of fear but a spirit of power and of love and of a sound mind. If there is a desire to progress in faith, progress in grace, progress toward the consummation of the age, there will have to be a constant stirring of faith.

John Wesley, as an early Methodist, caught a glimpse of GOD's love. He taught holiness, but he also taught perfect love, and this "perfect love" to the early Methodists was an experience. If you will read the lives of some of them, you will find this true.

Preaching to an antagonistic crowd at one time, John Wesley stepped down among them with a heart full of love, with eyes full of tears, and with a mouth full of arguments. Such a combination could not be resisted! This is why the early Methodists thrived, because men of this type were in the lead. This is real Pentecost—"'For out of the abundance of the heart the mouth speaks'" (Matthew 12:34). Glory to GOD! When the "abundance" came out, love and passion were with it, and sinners who came to fight Wesley lost their antagonism and remained to pray. Nothing can stand in the way of that burning fire in the breast, that fire that will believe for all things. No matter what the need for the sinner in Zion, or out of Zion, that love will reach out in faith.

> NOTHING CAN STAND IN THE WAY OF THAT BURNING FIRE IN THE BREAST, THAT FIRE THAT WILL BELIEVE FOR ALL THINGS.

OUR WALK OF FAITH

Beloved, the real love of GOD is like a flame of fire from heaven, and when it gets into your soul, it will work for others. The fire of heaven is brought from heaven by faith, and it works through us by faith.

Faith will reach out when there is love; but when there is little love, there is little faith. If you find yourself in a critical attitude towards yourself or toward others, you will find yourself with little love and with little faith, and you are in no

> **FAITH WILL REACH OUT WHEN THERE IS LOVE; BUT WHEN THERE IS LITTLE LOVE, THERE IS LITTLE FAITH.**

position to be of help to yourself or anyone else. But if you will humble yourself before the LORD and before them until love comes in, you will find yourself with faith, too, for faith works by love!

In 2 Thessalonians 1:3, we read Paul's words, "We are bound to thank GOD always for you, brethren, as it is fitting, because your faith grows exceedingly, and the love of every one of you all abounds toward each other." Paul sent Timothy to the Thessalonians to see how they were believing GOD, to see whether they were "believing believers" or "unbelieving believers." If they were believing GOD would meet them, then they would grow in every way. Here he writes that their faith was growing so that there was a charity and love among them. GOD met them. If we had Paul here today, he would examine our faith and, by this, measure our spiritual growth.

How is your faith? Faith pleases GOD—without faith it is impossible to please Him—and it is a wonderful thing when, because of the desire in the depths of our hearts to please Him, our faith reaches out to Him and to others, a faith that springs from love. CHRIST Himself demonstrated such a faith and a love when He faced and suffered the agonies of the cross.

CHRIST'S WORK

In the Garden of Gethsemane, JESUS CHRIST faced the rebellion of satan against GOD, the unbelief and all that Eve imbibed of the nature of the devil back in the Garden of Eden. He, who knew no sin, humbled Himself and imbibed that very nature. He said, "'O My FATHER, if it is possible, let this cup pass from Me; nevertheless, not as I will, but as You will'" (Matthew 26:39).

Beloved, your consecration can never compare to this consecration. Why did He do it? Love compelled Him. Love motivated Him just as love motivates our faith. He never could be my Substitute or yours unless He endured the cross. He not only took our sins, but He also took our ungodly, sinful, devilish natures to the cross with Him. And with our sins, He took all the results of our sins—our sicknesses, disease, and chastisement.

> **WHY DID HE DO IT? LOVE COMPELLED HIM. LOVE MOTIVATED HIM . . .**

To understand just what CHRIST accomplished in His work on the cross, let's go back to the Garden of Eden. There we see the first pair living in perfect innocence before GOD— knowing nothing of evil of any nature and enjoying every pleasant thing, especially the sweetness of fellowship with their Maker. But there came a day when satan through the serpent brought temptation to Eve. Satan in Genesis 3:1 talked to Eve through this serpent, and she innocently listened, "'Has GOD indeed said, "You shall not eat of every tree of the garden"?'"

There is so much in words. In drinking in the Word of GOD, we find that if we accept and open up to whatever His

Word says, we drink in His nature. If you want life, it is in His Word. If you want healing, it is in His Word. If you want Divine love, it is in the Word. If you want His will, it is in the Word. GOD expresses Himself, and if we listen with open hearts to His words, His nature will flow powerfully into us.

The same is true when an individual listens to the devil. This was the very thing that Eve did in her simplicity. She just drank in everything he said. In essence, he said, "You won't die if you eat of the tree. GOD doesn't want you to eat of it because He is hiding something from you that you should know."

> **GOD EXPRESSES HIMSELF, AND IF WE LISTEN WITH OPEN HEARTS TO HIS WORDS, HIS NATURE WILL FLOW POWERFULLY INTO US.**

The enemy beguiled her into listening to his subtle reasoning. In so doing, she imbibed the nature of satan himself.

Let us consider the nature Eve imbibed. We learn in Isaiah 14:12 something about the nature of the devil, Lucifer or the son of the morning. The Scripture tells us that because of pride satan was lifted up and endeavored to be greater than GOD. The determination was in his spirit to have himself exalted. Eve imbibed his nature of pride in her fallen state.

There is another feature about his nature that is expressed in this Scripture—his rejection of the Word of GOD. This was the very thing he injected into the heart, mind, and spirit of Eve. He bit her with the unbelief that was satanic. Again, he took a large company of the angels with him into a terrible rebellion. With this rebellion, he stung Eve in the Garden of Eden.

So you see today, when you consider human nature, it has that satanic nature that Eve received, and through Adam and Eve it spread to the generations that followed. Rebellion is in everyone—not just a common rebellion but a satanic rebellion in the spirit and in the nature.

The same is true in unbelief. It is satanic unbelief and satanic pride in the human being. As far as we are capable naturally, we can be as devilish as the devil himself. We could excuse it, look at it as some little thing that doesn't amount to much, but beloved, think of the depths of it, the awfulness of sin. The satanic nature is in the old creation wherever you find it.

> AS FAR AS WE ARE CAPABLE NATURALLY, WE CAN BE AS DEVILISH AS THE DEVIL HIMSELF.

The same rebellion that disturbed all of heaven, the same unbelief that disrupted the creation, the same pride that tries to bring GOD down from His throne is striking away today in the world. Is it any wonder it has wrecked the world the way it has? I would have been wrecked and everything around me before I was saved if it hadn't been for the grace of GOD withholding me. So would you. But thank GOD for grace.

Do you see this picture? Look at it very carefully, and let the SPIRIT OF GOD unfold it to you. Let us hit sin hard wherever we see it, especially when it manifests within us. Sometimes, we condone it and say we have a reason to behave so. We do have a reason if we want to live in the old creation. We have a reason to have a temper, a reason to be proud, a reason to have unbelief in our spirits if we want to live in the old creation. But, thank GOD, there is a better way.

Now, let us look again at the agony of JESUS in Gethsemane. Why the agony? Because the human JESUS was facing the cross? Was He agonizing because He was afraid He wouldn't be able to bear the awful load? No, it was GOD in awful agony in the Garden of Gethsemane. Oh, that hour—

that hour He drank that bitter cup. What was that cup? He became sin. That pure, spotless, holy One—that One who never had a sinful nature like you and me—became sin for us.

There was no sin in the blood stream of JESUS. There was no disease in His body. He was a perfect human, the same as Adam before the fall. He faced the same thing that Eve faced. That pure, spotless, undefiled nature humbled Himself, opened Himself up to become sin, to imbibe the nature of the devil himself, to take on Himself the pride, the selfishness, the awful unbelief and rebellion to the Kingdom of GOD. Not only to do this but to go into hell and taste the powers of eternal death. My sin and damnation He accepted in the Garden of Gethsemane. He opened up to it, separated from GOD—tasted eternal separation. He went through whatever any sinner could ever go through. JESUS opened up to it in the Garden of Gethsemane.

Gethsemane was not only the Garden of Agony; it was the Garden of Victory. Oh, the love of GOD! Oh, the wondrous work of CHRIST! What do we owe? How could we keep ignoring Him? How could we hold back our hearts from His?

He took my weaknesses, my sufferings, my sin, my guilt, my rebellion, my unbelief, my pride, my selfishness, my devilishness. The SON OF GOD, not man, but GOD agonized in Gethsemane. GOD went to hell, suffered hell, and tasted eternal death—to redeem us. Oh, the victory, the triumph over satan and all his powers. Hallelujah!

He was my Substitute. Oh, glory! He broke the powers of satanic sin in my life and satisfied a broken law, the righteous law of GOD. He took me through it, brought me out on top of the

> GOD WENT TO HELL, SUFFERED HELL, AND TASTED ETERNAL DEATH —TO REDEEM US.

world over all satanic power, and seated me in the heavenlies with JESUS—even there on the throne with Him. He is able to save to the uttermost. This is uttermost salvation!

And this He did motivated by love, demonstrating for us how love should motivate our faith. My faith attests to His great love, and my faith confesses, "I believe He died for me."

> AND THIS HE DID MOTIVATED BY LOVE, DEMONSTRATING FOR US HOW LOVE SHOULD MOTIVATE OUR FAITH.

7

"I BELIEVE" IS . . .

Faith's Confession

"But what does it say? 'The word is near you, in your mouth and in your heart' (that is, the word of faith which we preach): that if you confess with your mouth the LORD JESUS and believe in your heart that GOD has raised Him from the dead, you will be saved." (Romans 10:8-9)

G OD is especially interested in these days in producing faith in His children. We should, above all things, endeavor to encourage our faith in GOD. Anything that would discourage our faith, that would cut across our faith, we should hate and detest as we detest the venom of the serpent. We must see it as a means to rob us of the things of GOD, to rob us of the fellowship of the LORD, and to bring the displeasure of Him upon us.

> ANYTHING THAT WOULD DISCOURAGE OUR FAITH . . . WE SHOULD HATE AND DETEST . . . WE MUST SEE IT AS A MEANS TO ROB US OF THE THINGS OF GOD . . .

We know Hebrews 11:6 says, "But without faith it is impossible to please Him, for he who comes to GOD must believe that He is, and that He is a rewarder of those who diligently seek Him." Nothing brings us any more displeasure than to find that our friends and loved ones do not have confidence in us, that they do not believe in us. So it is with GOD, who is especially interested in bringing forth faith.

However, many Christians come under condemnation, and some seem to live there most of the time though the Bible declares, "There is therefore now no condemnation to those who are in CHRIST JESUS, who do not walk according to the flesh, but according to the SPIRIT" (Romans 8:1). I believe this, do you? Who is he that condemns? There is only One who can, and that is JESUS, and He doesn't! He died for us. He became our Substitute, bore our sins and our afflictions in His body on the tree. He bore our chastisement and our judgment, so He is our victory, our triumph, our all in all.

If we are to become overcomers, there must come a revolution in our Christian lives. We will have to come out of our inferiority complexes—our senses of failure, weakness, etc.—remembering we "can do all things through CHRIST who strengthens" us (Philippians 4:13).

Consider then Hebrews 3:1, "Therefore, holy brethren, partakers of the heavenly calling, consider the Apostle and High Priest of our confession, CHRIST JESUS." CHRIST is our confession; He is the High Priest of our confession. It is necessary to hold fast to Him and to our confession. We see this in Hebrews 4:14—"Seeing then that we have a great High Priest who has passed through the heavens, JESUS the SON OF GOD, let us hold fast our confession."

> **CHRIST IS OUR CONFESSION; HE IS THE HIGH PRIEST OF OUR CONFESSION.**

A RIGHT CONFESSION

The twelve spies made a confession when they returned to the children of Israel after viewing Canaan. They said it was a land flowing with milk and honey, a good land. But the ten said, "'We are not able to go up against the people, for they are stronger than we'" (Numbers 13:31). The two countered their fellow spies. They asserted that, though there were giants in the land, these were their bread (Numbers 14:9).

Here were two confessions—the right one was a confession of faith while the wrong one was a confession of unbelief. Two of them took a stand upon GOD's faithfulness and His integrity. They kept confessing faith and went into the land forty years afterward. But because of a wrong confession, the others died in the wilderness. The Scripture says, "So we see that they could not enter in because of unbelief" (Hebrews 3:19).

The same thing is going on today all around us. Some are making a right confession and others a wrong one. Beloved, we cannot make a wrong confession and get into the Promised Land.

> BELOVED, WE CANNOT MAKE A WRONG CONFESSION AND GET INTO THE PROMISED LAND.

What is a wrong confession? It is looking at situations, sizing them up by sense knowledge, going by our own judgments, measuring things by our own measurements, judging from what we see and hear and feel instead of judging things by the eternal, unchangeable, everlasting Word of GOD. For instance, in sickness, we say, "My aches," "My pains," or "My arthritis." What kind of confessions are these? Wrong indeed. GOD has stated in His Word that by His stripes we were healed. The work was finished at Calvary, and by His stripes, through faith, we are healed.

Beloved, remember the words of Paul:

> *If you confess with your mouth the LORD JESUS
> and believe in your heart that GOD has raised*

> *Him from the dead, you will be saved. For with*
> *the heart one believes unto righteousness, and*
> *with the mouth confession is made unto salva-*
> *tion. (Romans 10:9-10)*

OUR VICTORY

Two things will bring victory—heart faith and mouth confession. They are inseparable. My heart must respond to what GOD says because GOD says it. His Word is life-giving, powerful, and sharper than any two-edged sword. His Word is spirit and life, for it is eternally settled in heaven. Therefore, I can declare the same things that GOD declares, and He expects me to. His Word declares, "Therefore, if anyone is in CHRIST, he is a new creation" (2 Corinthians 5:17). In CHRIST, I am a new creation for GOD says I am, and I must take that stand. Sometimes, I have to say it over and over again, for I must "hold fast the confession of faith."

> TWO THINGS WILL
> BRING VICTORY—
> HEART FAITH AND
> MOUTH CONFESSION.
> THEY ARE INSEPARABLE.

It matters not how much the enemy would bring condemnation, for there is no condemnation to "those who are in CHRIST JESUS, who do not walk according to the flesh, but according to the SPIRIT." It is not what I feel but what GOD'S Word says. It does not say, "Confess with your mouth your sickness, your weakness, and everlasting failure." No! Rather, confess the LORD JESUS. Keep confessing Him. *Oh, JESUS, JESUS, I am reveling in all the provisions you have made for me.* Hallelujah! We must take this stand, even when we do not feel it.

We Pentecostal people have lived in blessings. It seems like these days we are in a transition period. We do not seem to have the blessing and anointings we used to have. Some of us do not know what to make of it. The devil tells us we are backslidden. By agreeing, "Yes, that must be right," I begin to feel backslidden because of a wrong confession. But a confession of faith would declare, "I am in JESUS, and I see my place in Him. I am as happy as can be." If only we could see it, there is an attitude, a position that will hold us steady and keep us under the favor and flow of the SPIRIT OF GOD.

Have you caught a vision of what JESUS is to you? What GOD has made Him to be for you? He is for you. All glory to His name!

Much of our difficulty is in our thinking, in our minds, but there is a provision made. We read of it in Romans 12:

> *I beseech you therefore, brethren, by the mercies of GOD, that you present your bodies a living sacrifice, holy, acceptable to GOD, which is your reasonable service. And do not be conformed to this world, but be transformed by the renewing of your mind, that you may prove what is that good and acceptable and perfect will of GOD. (1-2)*

Instead of having our minds weakness-conscious, self-conscious, failure-conscious, inferiority-conscious, and sickness-conscious, we can become GOD-conscious, the Word of GOD-conscious.

How does this come? How do we receive the renewing of the mind? By prayerfully meditating on the Word of GOD and by refusing to think of those former things anymore. Much of our preaching is only negative and keeps us in turmoil and disturbed. But standing on the Word of GOD that I am in JESUS gives the HOLY SPIRIT a chance to make the Word real, to make it practical, and to prove its fulfillment in my life.

The principles of faith work just as two and two make four. When, for example, our hearts give assent to believe a

> **THE PRINCIPLES OF FAITH WORK JUST AS TWO AND TWO MAKE FOUR.**

Scripture, and we say, "It is so," then we can go on our way rejoicing, and it is so! There comes a time when the heart lays hold on the Word, and with it there is a principle that grips you, and you know that what the Word says is true. You just know, and you know you know, but you don't know how you know! Praise the LORD!

Faith works best in the hard places and in the darkest places because they are the places in which we trust GOD most. It is characteristic of human nature that it does not trust GOD unless it has to.

> **FAITH WORKS BEST IN THE HARD PLACES AND IN THE DARKEST PLACES BECAUSE THEY ARE THE PLACES IN WHICH WE TRUST GOD MOST.**

We do not trust GOD much when we have everything. As long as we can get medicine, hospitalization, etc., it is hard to trust GOD for our healing. GOD is searching for faith. Without faith, it is impossible to please Him.

JESUS said, "'This is the work of GOD, that you believe in Him whom He sent'" (John 6:29). And the writer of Hebrews said, "Let us therefore be diligent to enter that rest." These Scriptures speak of work and labor. It is not always easy to believe, to always keep the heart attitude in the place where we can say, "Yes, LORD, I believe Your Word. I believe You in this trial. I believe Your Word in spite of everything that I see around me that contradicts it." As Paul told Timothy, we must "fight the good fight of faith" and "lay hold on eternal life" (1 Timothy 6:12).

GOD wants to bring His people to a place where He can trust them to walk with Him under any circumstances. When you give a heart assent to His Word, faith will work. It will every time!

SIGNS FOLLOWING

JESUS said, "'These signs will follow those who believe'" (Mark 16:17). People today are saying, "Where are the signs? Why don't the signs follow?" They talk about the good days and how backslidden we are today. LORD, help us! We cannot gain ground that way. Our part is to believe. "'These signs shall follow those who *believe.*'" I am a believer. This is my confession. I will not confess I am an unbeliever. The signs will follow us as we take the attitude, "LORD, I believe. Thank You, JESUS."

> THE SIGNS WILL FOLLOW US AS WE TAKE THE ATTITUDE, "LORD, I BELIEVE. THANK YOU, JESUS."

As I come believing and receiving, I rise above everything and am a victor over death, hell, and the grave through CHRIST. Let us take Him. Let us raise our hands in full surrender and say, "I take You, JESUS, for I am in You and by Your grace will hold fast the confession of faith for the fulfillment of every promise."

In ending this discussion of faith's confession, I am reminded of the great heroes of faith as recorded in Hebrews 11, and I must conclude with four powerful verses from that chapter:

> *And what more shall I say? For the time would fail me to tell of Gideon and Barak and Samson and Jephthah, also of David and Samuel and the prophets: who through faith subdued kingdoms, worked righteousness, obtained prom-*

ises, stopped the mouths of lions, quenched the violence of fire, escaped the edge of the sword, out of weakness were made strong, became valiant in battle, turned to flight the armies of the aliens. Women received their dead raised to life again. Others were tortured, not accepting deliverance, that they might obtain a better resurrection. (32-35)

Dear reader, I believe GOD! Let that be the confession of your faith, too, knowing that GOD's Presence is promised to those who believe!

8

GOD'S PRESENCE IS . . .
Faith's Promise

> *"And He said, 'My Presence will go with you,*
> *and I will give you rest.'" (Exodus 33:14)*

This is man's greatest need—the ever-glorious, all-powerful, loving, and perpetual Presence of GOD. For this purpose was man created: that he might enjoy communion and fellowship with his Creator. No matter what his repute, there is no real satisfaction without this abiding Presence to meet and satisfy the longings of his heart.

> THIS IS MAN'S GREATEST NEED— THE EVER-GLORIOUS, ALL-POWERFUL, LOVING, AND PERPETUAL PRESENCE OF GOD.

In the verse above, GOD was speaking to Moses concerning leaving Mount Sinai to lead a stubborn and stiff-necked people into the land of Canaan to fulfill the promise He had given many centuries before to their father, Abraham. GOD had promised His Angel to accompany Moses (Exodus 33:2), but Moses refused to be satisfied with this assurance, so his reply to GOD was, "'If Your Presence does not go with us, do not bring us up from here'" (Exodus 33:15). Since Moses had found favor with GOD, His Presence did go with them.

THE NEED FOR HIS PRESENCE

There were two reasons given by Moses for why he wanted

the Presence of GOD with him. He said,

> "For how then will it be known that Your peo-
> ple and I have found grace in Your sight, except
> You go with us? So we shall be separate, Your
> people and I, from all the people who are upon
> the face of the earth." (Exodus 33:16)

Moses desired that GOD be manifest in their midst to show other nations they were under GOD's grace. Also, His Presence would mean separation from all other peoples.

To experience the Presence of GOD in their midst was of great import. It brought an abundant supply of their daily, temporal needs; it was a protection from all the powers of evil and unpleasant climatic conditions which they would encounter. They would have the miracles of GOD in manifestation, and all their enemies would be subdued.

THE EXPERIENCE OF HIS PRESENCE

I praise the LORD for His marvelous Presence with us during the time that we have sojourned in Elim Bible Institute. How preciously has His Presence been manifested in multitudinous ways. We can but marvel in view of all His favors. Praise His matchless name!

During this time, we have witnessed some of His wonderful miracles and have been almost overwhelmed with inner spiritual blessings, as wave upon wave of joy, life, and glory has filled our hearts to overflowing. During this time, He has abundantly supplied our every temporal need. We have also enjoyed very much of His voice of prophecy giving us Divine wisdom and instruction.

As He has been with us during these past years, we can look to the future in full assurance and faith to His continued

Presence and fellowship as we individually are obedient to His will and humbly trust Him to be our abundant supply in everything.

You, too, are looking forward to the full inheritance of all that has been promised us for these last days and in the eternities.

I know that the world is setting before our young people great allurements of worldly opportunities in business, social, and even religious life, which are drawing many away from this high calling, and they are missing GOD'S best. Only as your heart is occupied with JESUS and you love Him dearly, having no other desire but the sweetness and the glories of His Presence and communion, will you be able to find your way through the allurements and entanglements of this present hour.

So I would admonish you to be ever watchful of your prayer life and your aptitudes in the perusal and study of His precious Word. Also, abandon yourselves to live in His anointing and the ministries which He so graciously bestows upon you. By so doing, JESUS will be lifted up, His very Presence in all His fullness will be realized with you, and you shall have His approval through this life and hear, "Well done, thou good and faithful servant," as you enter the life hereafter.

> AS HE HAS BEEN WITH US DURING THESE PAST YEARS, WE CAN LOOK TO THE FUTURE IN FULL ASSURANCE AND FAITH . . .

> ONLY AS YOUR HEART IS OCCUPIED WITH JESUS AND YOU LOVE HIM DEARLY . . . WILL YOU BE ABLE TO FIND YOUR WAY THROUGH THE ALLUREMENTS AND ENTANGLEMENTS OF THIS PRESENT HOUR.

THE PROMISE OF HIS PRESENCE

Recently, as I was reminiscing about GOD'S leadings and dealings in the past times of discipline as well as times of visitation and outpouring of His SPIRIT—I took from the promise box this Scripture text, "'As I was with Moses, so I will be with you'" (Joshua 1:5). I was much encouraged as I considered the way in which GOD moved in the life of this chosen leader of Israel.

In our first chapter, we discussed this verse, "He made known His ways to Moses, His acts to the children of Israel" (Psalm 103:7). I was stirred with a fresh hunger in my heart to be so intimately acquainted with GOD that I, too, would understand His ways as well as behold His acts. As we've discussed already, it is very important to have an understanding of what GOD is doing and to know His purposes in His acts.

> ... IT IS VERY IMPORTANT TO HAVE AN UNDERSTANDING OF WHAT GOD IS DOING AND TO KNOW HIS PURPOSES IN HIS ACTS.

In reading the book of Deuteronomy, we find Moses explaining the ways of GOD to the children of Israel as he goes over the journeyings of Israel from Egypt through the wilderness to the border of Canaan. GOD explains through Moses the reason for the many experiences through which He led them.

It is wonderful to have GOD take time with us and to explain His purposes in our various experiences after we have gone through them. Thus, we learn many wonderful lessons of the ways and plans of GOD in our individual lives. We also see how merciful and faithful He has been to us, even though we have been so void of understanding and many times have failed Him so miserably in our stubbornness and unbelief.

Looking again at the record in Deuteronomy, we see how GOD had entered with Israel into every detail of their daily lives. He daily fed them with manna and gave them water from the rock. His resources, both temporal and spiritual, were always abundant and graciously supplied to meet their every need. They were ever encouraged by His lovingkindness to draw upon these abundant resources. He sought in this always to encourage and increase their faith.

He does the same with us today. We find that the "all things" of GOD's appointments in our lives are to teach us to trust Him wholly and to appropriate His abundances! Without faith, it is impossible to please Him. Faith is a very precious grace, for it is more valuable than silver or gold.

> **WE FIND THAT THE "ALL THINGS" OF GOD'S APPOINTMENTS IN OUR LIVES ARE TO TEACH US TO TRUST HIM WHOLLY AND TO APPROPRIATE HIS ABUNDANCES!**

Hear the words of Moses to Israel as recorded in Deuteronomy 8:2-6.

"And you shall remember that the LORD your GOD led you all the way these forty years in the wilderness, to humble you and test you, to know what was in your heart, whether you would keep His commandments or not. So He humbled you, allowed you to hunger, and fed you with manna which you did not know nor did your fathers know, that He might make you know that man shall not live by bread alone; but man lives by every word that proceeds from the mouth of the LORD. Your gar-

> *ments did not wear out on you, nor did your*
> *foot swell these forty years. You should know in*
> *your heart that as a man chastens his son, so*
> *the LORD your GOD chastens you. Therefore*
> *you shall keep the commandments of the LORD*
> *your GOD, to walk in His ways and to fear Him."*

So today, GOD has arranged and ordered for His people paths that bring severe testing. Often we hear the question, "Why does the LORD have to try us so?" Paul gives us a definite answer in these words—"All things work together for good to those who love GOD, to those who are the called according to His purpose" (Romans 8:28). This should explain the "why."

In Israel's case, it was to humble them and to prove them —that they might know what was in their hearts. Is that not our need today? How wicked are the tendencies of the human heart, and how void of the virtues of JESUS. If we were left to go our own ways, we surely would become proud, arrogant, self-assertive, and independent.

> HOW WICKED ARE THE
> TENDENCIES OF THE
> HUMAN HEART, AND
> HOW VOID OF THE
> VIRTUES OF JESUS.

My dear reader, it is most evident that severe testings and provings are needed to bring about the same results in those who received of GOD in the visitation which GOD so graciously brought to us over the years. Misunderstandings, dis-fellowships, prejudices, and criticisms are manifest so much everywhere because men are seeking their own and not the things of CHRIST.

How faithful GOD is to deal with us in His mercy, by discipline and teaching. He desires to bring forth the peaceable fruit of righteousness in our hearts and lives. If we will learn the lessons He desires to teach us in these varied experiences, we will become enriched in our own spiritual lives and will be made a rich blessing to the Church and world and will also satisfy GOD'S great heart of love.

We never would have known how needy we were had not GOD taken such pains to prove us and let us see our heart's need for His ever-abiding Presence. We never would have known our need and the great resources of our GOD had we not been brought to the end of our own resources and strength.

> WE NEVER WOULD HAVE KNOWN OUR NEED AND THE GREAT RESOURCES OF OUR GOD HAD WE NOT BEEN BROUGHT TO THE END OF OUR OWN RESOURCES AND STRENGTH.

How like Israel we have murmured and complained and wandered in our wildernesses, but still heaven's manna has fallen, and the water from the rock still flows. Hallelujah!

GOD took such great pains with Israel because He had such a glorious future for them. How marvelous were His plans for them in the land of Canaan and, in fact, for the future centuries in their MESSIAH. Even in the return of CHRIST and through the millennial age, GOD'S purposes will still be manifest in and through Israel in great blessing.

This should speak to us of GOD'S great purposes for *us* in *our* future, for we are promised that as we abide in Him, He will abide in us. His abiding Presence is affirmed throughout the Scriptures. JESUS Himself promised His disciples, "'And lo, I am with you always, even to the end of the age'" (Matthew 28:20).

Even when JESUS spoke of His leaving the earth, He assured His disciples by saying,

> *"If you love Me, keep My commandments. And I will pray the FATHER, and He will give you another HELPER, that He may abide with you forever—the SPIRIT OF TRUTH, whom the world cannot receive, because it neither sees Him nor knows Him; but you know Him, for He dwells with you and will be in you. I will not leave you orphans; I will come to you." (John 14:15-18)*

Here is His promise of the precious HOLY SPIRIT. As we place our faith in the SON OF GOD and in His Word, we experience the indwelling, ever-abiding Presence of His HOLY SPIRIT. GOD greatly desires that we might come into all of His fullness and that JESUS might be manifest in the riches of His grace, power, and glory in us, so that in His return we may be like Him. But this will require some schooling, as it were.

9

C H R I S T ' S   P O V E R T Y   I S . . .

Faith's School

"For you know the grace of our LORD JESUS CHRIST,
that though He was rich, yet for your sakes He became poor,
that you through His poverty might become rich."
(2 Corinthians 8:9)

"Through His poverty"—what does this mean? That He, the LORD of earth and heaven, the Creator of all, dispossessed Himself of all earthly and heavenly possessions, that the riches of earth and heaven might be ours. It means this and very much more.

Is through His poverty something for Him alone or something in which His disciples are to share? Let us prayerfully consider this precious nugget of Divine truth.

> COULD IT NOT BE THAT THE CHURCH HAS FORGOTTEN WHAT IT IS TO BE "POOR IN SPIRIT" YET RICH IN CHRIST?

Today, the Church everywhere practices the right to possess and enjoy the riches of earth. She is rich and increased with goods as evidenced everywhere, and she often boasts of this as an evidence of spirituality. Could it not be that the Church has forgotten what it is to be "poor in spirit" yet rich in CHRIST?

ITS MEANING

In seeking to understand CHRIST's poverty, let us first turn and gaze on our blessed LORD. He might have lived upon this earth with wealth and had the joy of distributing to the needy. Or He might have come into the world with moderate means, had a home where He could have laid His head, and not have had to live a dependent life. But He could not be in any of these positions and be our precious SAVIOR. There was a Divine necessity that His life must be one of entire and complete poverty. There were many reasons for this as we shall see.

> THERE WAS A DIVINE NECESSITY THAT HIS LIFE MUST BE ONE OF ENTIRE AND COMPLETE POVERTY.

First of all, we must recognize CHRIST'S poverty was part of His entire and deep humiliation. He had to descend to the lowest depths of our own human misery and to share all the consequences of sin to be our SAVIOR. In all ages, the poor have been despised. JESUS came to the despised. CHRIST'S poverty has ever been counted one of the proofs of His love. Love delights in giving—perfect love in giving all.

> TO MULTITUDES OF NEEDY PEOPLE, EARTHLY NEEDS WERE AND ARE . . . AN OCCASION FOR HEAVENLY HELP, THE SCHOOL FOR A LIFE OF FAITH, THE KNOWLEDGE OF GOD'S FAITHFULNESS, AND THE PATH TO HEAVENLY RICHES.

Most people have to struggle with poverty. The majority of the world's troubles can be traced to the struggle against poverty. The majority of saints have been poor and afflicted people. To multitudes of needy people, earthly needs were and are to them an occasion for heavenly help, the school for a life of faith, the knowledge of GOD'S faithfulness, and the path to heavenly riches.

His poverty was also the proof of His complete victory over the world. He was not bound in any way by His wealth.

His Kingdom was not of this world. In the wilderness, satan could not tempt Him with all the riches of the world.

There were still deeper meanings of CHRIST'S spiritual poverty. It was a school of training for the SON OF MAN. As a man, He had to learn obedience by the things He suffered.

Poverty is ever a trial. Poverty implies dependence upon others. It means contempt and shame. It brings want and human suffering. Our blessed LORD felt all these as a man. He proved through poverty His submission to the will of the FATHER and His absolute trust in Him.

> HE PROVED THROUGH POVERTY HIS SUBMISSION TO THE WILL OF THE FATHER AND HIS ABSOLUTE TRUST IN HIM.

It was part of His school of faith. In His own life, He had to prove that GOD and the riches of heaven can more than satisfy a man who has nothing on earth.

His poverty was one of the marks of His entire separation from the world. This was an essential element of His wholly perfect life—one great secret of His power to conquer and to save.

OUR SCHOOL

How do we have a share in this poverty of CHRIST? What did JESUS mean when He said to His disciples, "Follow Me"? He called them to share in His poor and homeless life, in His entire dependence on the care of GOD and in the kindness of men. He often referred to forsaking all, renouncing all, losing all, and they understood this and manifested it by forsaking their nets and customs and saying through Peter, "'See we have left all and followed You'" (Matthew 19:27).

With them, as with Him, the surrender of all property and the acceptance of a state of poverty was their call. This was the inner circle of His disciples. Not all of His followers had this call in His day, neither so at the present. One reason for this was because many could not bear it and cannot today. Wealth and prosperity with all their blessings can ensnare us. They can force us from a dependent life of faith. As a result of this, no law can be laid down for each to follow. It is not a question of law but of liberty.

Too often Christian liberty is spoken of as the freedom from sacrifice of our own will or the enjoyment of earthly things. Its real meaning is the very opposite. True love asks to be as free as possible from self and the world that it might bring all to GOD. It is not how far I can go as a Christian, still free to do this or the other. A truly free spirit purposes to follow CHRIST to the uttermost. The man who really gives up all of earthly possession because he sets his heart upon the treasures in heaven can count upon GOD to provide the necessities of earth.

> THE MAN WHO REALLY GIVES UP ALL OF EARTHLY POSSESSION BECAUSE HE SETS HIS HEART UPON THE TREASURES IN HEAVEN CAN COUNT UPON GOD TO PROVIDE THE NECESSITIES OF EARTH.

We read in Matthew 6:24, "'No one can serve two masters; for either he will hate the one and love the other, or else he will be loyal to the one and despise the other. You cannot serve GOD and mammon.'" The great majority of Christian people are in servitude to money. They're in debt and are consumed with getting out of it while they continue to create more.

The twenty-fifth verse of Matthew 6 exhorts us, "'Do not worry about your life, what you will eat or what you will drink; nor about your body, what you will put on. Is not life more than food and the body more than clothing?'" Take no anxious thought. You cannot have real faith in GOD and be anxious at one and the same time, for—

> *"Which of you by worrying can add one cubit to his stature? So why do you worry about clothing? Consider the lilies of the field, how they grow: they neither toil nor spin; and yet I say to you that even Solomon in all his glory was not arrayed like one of these. Now if GOD so clothes the grass of the field, which today is, and tomorrow is thrown into the oven, will He not much more clothe you, O you of little faith? Therefore do not worry, saying, 'What shall we eat?' or 'What shall we drink?' or 'What shall we wear?' For after all these things the Gentiles seek. For your heavenly FATHER knows that you need all these things. But seek first the kingdom of GOD and His righteousness, and all these things shall be added to you." (Matthew 6:27-33)*

It is also written, "My GOD shall supply all your need according to His riches in glory by CHRIST JESUS" (Philippians 4:19). Men with the best intentions may fail, and human promises, alas, are sometimes forgotten, but GOD never fails the trusting heart, and His promises cannot be broken.

> . . . HUMAN PROMISES, ALAS, ARE SOMETIMES FORGOTTEN, BUT GOD NEVER FAILS THE TRUSTING HEART, AND HIS PROMISES CANNOT BE BROKEN.

Let us lift our eyes heavenward and see who GOD is. He desires to establish and build up His children in faith to stem the tide of their seeking after natural things. While the believer is trusting, the LORD is providing and, at the same time, imparting strength and life to him.

JESUS wants to live His life again through us—to live His life of humiliation and abandonment to the will of GOD in faith. He wants to school our faith through our understanding His poverty—that we would be wholly dependent upon GOD in sweet fellowship and communion. This is the life of great blessing and the only really enjoyable life for man to live. This is a life of heavenly reality where JESUS is our all in all, where we are wholly devoted to Him.

> HE WANTS TO SCHOOL OUR FAITH THROUGH OUR UNDERSTANDING HIS POVERTY—THAT WE WOULD BE WHOLLY DEPENDENT UPON GOD IN SWEET FELLOWSHIP AND COMMUNION.

OUR DEVOTION

Leviticus 27:28 reads, ""Every devoted offering is most holy to the LORD."'" The word devoted is *cherem* in the Hebrew. It is translated in Scripture as accursed, accursed thing, curse, cursed thing, dedicated thing, destruction, destroy, devoted, and devoted thing.

It is difficult to conceive a word that seems to have two opposite meanings. For instance, when we think of the word accursed in our English language, we think of something GOD has doomed for destruction or judgment. When we think of something devoted, on the other hand, we consider such a thing held in sacred trust and ownership by Him.

As I understand it, *cherem* is a place or thing given into the hand of GOD, for His disposal according to His will or as He may have foreordained to destroy or keep as a sacred treasure. It is entirely His choice. It is something that He chooses to cut off from common use in perpetual consecration to His service. As Leviticus 27:28 reads in full:

"'Nevertheless no devoted offering that a man may devote to the LORD of all that he has, both man and beast, or the field of his possession, shall be sold or redeemed; every devoted offering is most holy to the LORD.'"

In this Scripture, we find certain possessions that have been consecrated to the LORD. They were reserved for Him even after the Year of Jubilee, when usually all possessions returned to their former owners. GOD had claims upon certain properties that He reserved for Himself alone.

Another passage using *cherem* is found in Joshua 6. The King James Version reads:

> **GOD HAD CLAIMS UPON CERTAIN PROPERTIES THAT HE RESERVED FOR HIMSELF ALONE.**

And the city shall be accursed [cherem], even it, and all that are therein, to the LORD: only Rahab the harlot shall live, she and all that are with her in the house, because she hid the messengers that we sent. And ye, in any wise keep yourselves from the accursed thing [cherem], lest ye make yourselves accursed, when ye take of the accursed thing, and make the camp of Israel a curse, and trouble it. But all the silver, and gold, and vessels of brass and iron, are consecrated unto the LORD: they shall come into the treasury of the LORD. (17-19)

In this context, the city mentioned is Jericho at the time when Israel moved into Canaan. Under the instruction of the

LORD which He gave to Joshua, they were to march around the city seven days, and on the seventh day, the walls would fall down flat. GOD told them particularly that all the spoil of the city, even the gold and the silver and vessels of brass and iron, belonged to Him and was to come into His treasury.

The children of Israel could have well considered that the spoil of war naturally belonged to the conquerors, and they as soldiers could have gathered it for themselves, but not so in this case. GOD, in a sense, said to them, "Hands off. All that the city has and holds belongs to Me, to dispose of as I please. I can take of its treasure into My sanctuary, and I can utterly destroy whatever portion I desire." Usually, the spoil of battle belonged to the army that won, but not so in the taking of Jericho. It all belonged to the LORD.

> **USUALLY, THE SPOIL OF BATTLE BELONGED TO THE ARMY THAT WON, BUT NOT SO IN THE TAKING OF JERICHO. IT ALL BELONGED TO THE LORD.**

There was one man in the army of the LORD that evidently did not heed what GOD had said. He saw a goodly Babylonish garment and a wedge of gold. He coveted, took, and hid them. Israel could get no farther in the conquest of Canaan till Achan, the covetous man, and all his family were destroyed. Many an Achan, who touches that which has been consecrated to GOD, will perish at the hand of the LORD in these last days.

This thought of absolute abandonment to another seems to have been quite common among many peoples down through the ages. This was especially true among the Romans —that one man would give himself for another in complete consecration, in devotion for a curse or a blessing. There were many who gave themselves to the king as a slave with no thought of ever having anything to say for themselves again.

CHRIST'S DEVOTION

When we consider the life and sacrifice of JESUS, we get the true import of *cherem*. JESUS CHRIST was GOD'S *cherem*. He was GOD'S devoted; He was GOD'S accursed. "For it is written, 'Cursed is everyone who hangs on a tree'" (Galatians 3:13). JESUS was our Substitute and bore the curse of the law of GOD which we had broken.

In His life, He was also GOD'S bond slave. He said, "'I always do those things that please Him'" (John 8:29). His school of learning was faith's school where He learned obedience through the things He suffered.

We see the Apostle Paul's emulation of CHRIST as he called himself the bond slave of the LORD. He wished himself accursed for his brethren if they might be saved. If our consecration and devotion are complete, we will be brought to such a place of faith and obedience that there will never be the slightest resistance to His will for us. We will so love Him that we will be as happy to have His curse as His blessing, and we will be willing to experience His poverty.

> **WHAT A POWER, THEN, THIS POVERTY OF CHRIST BECOMES, OPERATING IN OUR LIVES TO BRING RICHES TO OTHERS.**

What a power, then, this poverty of CHRIST becomes, operating in our lives to bring riches to others. His poverty in His people brings great blessing to others. Christian giving will not only be more liberal in amount but liberal in spirit.

Let us now ask a few questions. Do we know what this poverty is? Can we attain it? Are we willing to become poverty stricken?

In answer, we would say it surely takes the LORD in His dealings by the SPIRIT to work this in us. Sometimes, we may have to say, "LORD, I can't give this up, but You can take it from me." His grace is sufficient in this as well as in other things. We have GOD's perfect love for us and in us to work out His perfect will. And this, no doubt, will enable us to lay down our things and our very lives for CHRIST's sake.

10

THE CRUCIFIED LIFE IS . . .
The Life of Faith

"'I have been crucified with CHRIST; it is no longer I who live, but CHRIST lives in me; and the life which I now live in the flesh I live by faith in the SON OF GOD, who loved me and gave Himself for me.'" (Galatians 2:20)

The life of CHRIST was the crucified life. JESUS, who was wholly offered up to the will of GOD, as we discussed in chapter five, gave Himself as a voluntary offering to make atonement for the sins of the people. Indeed, His suffering was entirely voluntary. He laid down His life for us. Praise His precious name!

As the crucified life is typical of JESUS, so it also speaks to us of those that follow the LAMB whithersoever He goes and who take the way of sacrifice and crucifixion

> IN ORDER FOR HIS BRIDE TO SHARE HIS THRONE, SHE MUST KNOW THE PATH OF ABSOLUTE ABANDONMENT AND YIELDEDNESS TO HIM IN ALL THINGS . . .

that they may be to His honor, praise, and glory. In order for His Bride to share His throne, she must know the path of absolute abandonment and yieldedness to Him in all things, that she may be conformed to His image and ways.

CHRIST—THE BURNT OFFERING

The crucified CHRIST was the burnt offering made for our

atonement. He was the LAMB slain from the foundations of the world. And He personally was and is our burnt offering.

The fire's burning up the offering speaks to us of the suffering of the cross which He endured to atone for the sins of the people. The Hebrew word from whence we get the words, "burnt offering," means "that which goes up." It attests to this surrender of the complete sacrifice. It was the smoke from the sacrifice coming into the nostrils of GOD which was a sweet savor unto Him. In our day, we are more occupied with that which comes down. We are continually looking for a blessing to satisfy us, when our choicest thought should be that He would be satisfied with us.

We often lift our hands and open them. The position they are in shows whether there springs from our hearts a yieldedness to Him in worship or whether we are expecting Him to drop something into them. If we would only joyfully allow Him to put us through the fire, and in the midst of it praise Him, it would be a sweet odor unto Him.

> IF WE WOULD ONLY JOYFULLY ALLOW HIM TO PUT US THROUGH THE FIRE, AND IN THE MIDST OF IT PRAISE HIM, IT WOULD BE A SWEET ODOR UNTO HIM.

Again, I cannot stress this enough. His was a voluntary offering. It speaks of us who should put our confidence and trust in Him, surrendering entirely our wills to Him in all things. GOD never compels us against our wills, but He works in us to will and to do of His good pleasure.

Back to the sacrifice, it is important to note that it was first flayed or skinned. JESUS, as He hung upon the cross, was naked and open before the world. He had nothing that He withheld from humanity, if mankind would only receive it. His nature was practically open. So it is with us: We can have nothing hidden or covered, but we must be open before Him.

The carcass was then cut in pieces and placed upon the fire. In all of the other offerings, parts were saved for the priests and Levites but not so in the burnt offering: All must go up in the fire; nothing saved. So all our being must undergo real crucifixion.

JESUS said, "'Unless a grain of wheat falls into the ground and dies, it remains alone; but if it dies, it produces much grain'" (John 12:24) and again, "'If anyone desires to come after Me, let him deny himself, and take up his cross, and follow Me'" (Matthew 16:24). The general idea of self-denial is to deny yourself of something that you like, but true self-denial is to deny self. This can only be done by the SPIRIT's working in us real crucifixion.

Some specific parts of the carcass are mentioned. The head especially must be crucified. How much our heads get in the way of the SPIRIT OF GOD. Our fleshly reasoning, imagining, and mental training run on in a stream of natural life which is contrary to the stream of life in the SPIRIT, thus hindering GOD in so many ways. If the SPIRIT OF GOD has His way in our minds, there will be a casting down of our imaginations, reasonings, and everything that exalts itself against the knowledge of GOD—bringing into captivity every thought to the obedience of JESUS CHRIST.

> THE GENERAL IDEA OF SELF-DENIAL IS TO DENY YOURSELF OF SOMETHING THAT YOU LIKE, BUT TRUE SELF-DENIAL IS TO DENY SELF. THIS CAN ONLY BE DONE BY THE SPIRIT'S WORKING IN US REAL CRUCIFIXION.

The fat is also mentioned. This speaks to us of that which is sweet and naturally satisfying in our natures and make-up. Some people are naturally very sweet and congenial, and many are cultivated to be such. But as the LORD has His way in us and puts us in tests and trials, we may find that this is only a camouflage. We often are exposed as to what we really are, and those about us see and know our actual state.

The innards and the legs are especially mentioned with the thought that they were to be washed first with pure water. GOD must first deal in a special way with our inner affections, desires, motives, etc. There is a washing in water by the Word which cleanses us.

To be delivered from the sin in our inner lives which only GOD can see, however, we must undergo the fire. How the human heart casts its affections on human beings and things which are perfectly legitimate. But often as a result, others have first place and JESUS second, or possibly He is crowded out entirely, and many times we are not conscious that this is the case.

> TO BE DELIVERED FROM THE SIN IN OUR INNER LIVES WHICH ONLY GOD CAN SEE . . . WE MUST UNDERGO THE FIRE.

What intense sufferings and separations GOD'S people often have to be carried through in order to be brought into the place where JESUS completely fills their vision and satisfies. Many of GOD'S people have started out to follow Him in a splendid way; then, their hearts have opened up to someone or something in a natural way, and as a result, the devil has tripped them up, and they have lost their way. Many young people through human attachments of heart affection miss their call and spend a life of waywardness and separation from GOD'S first will and choice. I am reminded of these precious words —"When fingers cling, they sorrow bring into the loving heart. Crown JESUS king in every thing from all thy idols part."

Sometimes, we think that our motives are pure and our

desires spring from the LORD, but remember the human heart is deceptive. It is possible that our motives spring partly, at least, from our own human volitions. As a result, there is a mixture in our workings and ways and even in our service for Him. We should request that He wash us without and within, purging with fire if need be, "no matter how, if only sin, die out in me, die out in me."

The legs speak of our daily walk with the LORD. These, too, are washed with water. GOD must have a people that walk before each other in submission and before Him in holiness.

If we walk in the SPIRIT, we will not fulfill the lusts of the flesh. How much reproach is brought to bear upon the cause of CHRIST because of a waywardness of GOD'S people. But the true Bride of CHRIST will really come to walk in His ways and completely follow His steps. Let us pray these days, "Search me, O GOD, and know my heart; try me, and know my anxieties; and see if there is any wicked way in me, and lead me in the way everlasting" (Psalm 139:23-24). Remember, the LORD loves a broken and contrite heart (Psalm 51:17).

OUR DEATH—OUR OFFERING

The brokenness of you and me—here is the gate to all spiritual progress. Death must come, death to flesh and our own ways and struggles and what we are by nature—letting JESUS live out His life in us.

> **THE BROKENNESS OF YOU AND ME—HERE IS THE GATE TO ALL SPIRITUAL PROGRESS.**

We cannot raise a crop with such insects as caterpillars, locusts, and the like devouring them. There are insects in spiritual things also, such as pride, self-righteousness, and unbelief.

The wheat must fall into the ground and die. We have an

example of a young girl who came to our Bible school when she had the opportunity to go to another Bible school that could offer her nicer things than we could offer her.

One day, I asked her just why she came to our school. She said, "Because you teach the crucified life in this school." That sounded good from a young girl. I saw she wanted something deeper. She saw a laid down life and saw its value. Everything that comes from GOD calls to us for sacrifice and crucifixion.

If you and I don't catch that vision, we won't get much from Him.

> **EVERYTHING THAT COMES FROM GOD CALLS TO US FOR SACRIFICE AND CRUCIFIXION.**

I am reminded of a young man who was in Camp Meeting a few years ago. This young fellow did something in a meeting that was evidently out of order. Someone broke out in prophecy or interpretation and said something about the bad odor of the flesh. There was probably a lot of flesh in that meeting. The young man didn't have to take this word to heart if it didn't belong to him. But apparently he felt some of its heat applicable as he left and never returned.

Don't you see what it means? Don't you see what GOD is calling for? When the test comes, we don't die. Like the young man who left the meeting, we don't let go and lay down our lives. We still maintain our ways. Job got beyond that, however. The thought which impresses me in the book of Job is what satan said to GOD:

> *"Does Job fear GOD for nothing? Have You not made a hedge around him, around his household, and around all that he has on every side? You have blessed the work of his hands, and his possessions have increased in the land." (1:9-10)*

Satan was implying that Job would serve GOD only for the benefits He provided him. But GOD's response was to allow satan to prove Job. Job, consequently, was stripped of everything, and when satan got through with him, his eyes were still on the LORD. Satan had proved to him that the grace of GOD went beyond the natural.

Even JESUS had a marvelous ministry for the first eighteen months or two years, and then opposition began to arise, and He began to tell of His coming death at Calvary. Scripture says, "From that time many of His disciples went back and walked with Him no more. Then JESUS said to the twelve, 'Do you also want to go away?'" (John 6:66-67).

If there is ever a time when these Scriptures and truths should be put to the test, it is today. The ones that continue with GOD in faith are the ones that find the path of self-emptying—CHRIST in you,

> THE ONES THAT CONTINUE WITH GOD IN FAITH ARE THE ONES THAT FIND THE PATH OF SELF-EMPTYING . . .

the Hope of glory, reigning over the flesh. Are you willing to come down that fruit might be produced—fruit that remains?

OUR OFFERINGS TO GLORIFY GOD

Psalm 115:1 reads, "Not unto us, O LORD, not unto us, but unto Your name give glory, because of Your mercy, because of Your truth." There are two outstanding thoughts in this verse which I wish to bring to light—first, the insignificance and nothingness of man, and second, the greatness of GOD.

I suppose some of us who came up through denominational teaching remember the catechism we learned when we were children. One question was, "What is the chief aim of man?" The answer was, "To glorify GOD and to enjoy Him forever." And another was, "Why was man created?" The answer was, "For the glory of GOD." If this principle could get into your spirits and natures, the truth of it would surely settle a great many of your difficulties and problems.

With these thoughts that you were created only for the glory of GOD and the chief aim of your life was to glorify Him, forever foremost in your spirits, you would not be up when circumstances are favorable and down when they are unfavorable. In other words, if you were expecting GOD to get all the glory, you would have no reason to be down in the dumps because of disappointment. One great reason why you get discouraged is because you thought you were going to get something yourself. You were expecting to get a pat on the back, perhaps, and when you did not get it, you were disappointed. In every experience of life, whether good or bad, this thought should be uppermost, "LORD, right here, may in this situation my sole purpose be that You shall have all the glory."

> "LORD, RIGHT HERE, MAY IN THIS SITUATION MY SOLE PURPOSE BE THAT YOU SHALL HAVE ALL THE GLORY."

You did not come into this world by your own volition; you are not going out by your own choice. The LORD has His hand upon you. If you and I do not come into the place where we want Him, where we desire most of all that He will get the glory, we will miss the best of life. We will miss God, the reward before us, and doubtless make life miserable for ourselves and all who are around us because we have looked for something that God, in His plan and purpose, never meant for us.

To be sure, it is only as we live in the SPIRIT that we can glorify GOD and give Him the praise and honor that is due His name. The LORD alone, by the SPIRIT, can produce that which will satisfy the longings of His heart. Today, the world is full of service and of the exaltation of man who is doing something. May I remind you that that is the path on which the antichrist will ride to victory and triumph.

Then, this second thought, "Not unto us, O LORD, not unto us, but to Your name give glory." There has to be a denial of self, a continual refusal to ever allow anything to load itself upon you that would exalt your natural life. How nice it feels to the flesh to have someone smooth it over, to pat you on the back. But, beloved, the heart that is crying out for the plan and purpose of GOD will shrink from this. GOD never expected anything of the natural man but failure as far as spiritual and eternal things are con-

> GOD NEVER EXPECTED ANYTHING OF THE NATURAL MAN BUT FAILURE AS FAR AS SPIRITUAL AND ETERNAL THINGS ARE CONCERNED.

cerned. Just as long as you live in your natural state and are expecting something from yourselves, you are failing GOD.

One meaning of the word, "sin," is "missing the mark." Some try to see how far they can go before missing the mark. Our goal, however, should be that God be glorified every hour of our lives. When we miss that, it pains GOD, and we are sinners. I do not care how much experience you have had. Good old-fashioned Godly repentance is needed today for all self-centeredness and desires that heap upon us and that would pamper and satisfy the flesh. "Not unto us, O LORD, not

> GOOD OLD-FASHIONED GODLY REPENTANCE IS NEEDED TODAY FOR ALL SELF-CENTEREDNESS . . .

unto us, but unto Thy name give glory, for Thy mercy, and for Thy truth's sake," as the King James Version says.

So many times, Christians get into experiences of disappointment because they fail. That should not concern them. Perhaps, it is for GOD'S glory that they seem to be failures. In such a case, you should cry to GOD, "LORD, in this experience, if I have been a failure, somehow get glory to Your name!" When you pray like this, you will find GOD working, for He is jealous of His name.

Our text was written at a time of Israel's backsliding. Look at her in her times of blessing when GOD led her out of Egypt and through the wilderness. Look at His manifestation, the opening of the Red Sea, the marvelous deliverances from the powers of the enemy. Look at the grand and glorious supply of all their needs—the manna from heaven and the water from the rock.

GOD was ever there, continually manifesting Himself. But it seems there came a time when the heathen in a sneering way, because the supernatural was not manifest, were looking on, saying, "Where is their GOD?" You can consider the same today. Look at the great outpouring of the HOLY SPIRIT in the early church. The world knows of the great principles for which Christianity stood, and they also say, "Where is their GOD?" GOD will never get a chance to rise up unless you begin to pray as David the psalmist prayed.

I believe Pentecostalism in not in the state it once was. We Pentecostals should ask ourselves, "Where are we today?" We would doubtless answer, "We're not on fire as we used to be." The power of GOD is not manifest like it once was.

We are in a time of drought. The heathen are looking on, and they are saying, "Where is their GOD?" We should take the same attitude as the psalmist—"Not unto us, O LORD, not unto us, but to Your name give glory, because of Your mercy, because of Your truth."

We cannot plead our goodness nor anything else, not even some of the promises, because we have not kept the precepts of the LORD. We have dishonored Him. *LORD, in the depth of my heart I cry, "O GOD! Not unto me, but unto You, unto Your name be the glory."* Oh, the pleading, the strength of a prayer of that kind reaches GOD when other prayers fail. "Unto Your name be all the glory."

GOD wants to work, wants to be loosed. Look at Samson's experiences and see the marvelous power GOD put on him in his early life. For a number of reasons, he lost out. But there was a time when he was called to that great theater to make a play for a multitude of the lords of the Philistines. There was a cry that came forth in the heart of Samson that day that caused him to say he wanted to feel the pillars of the temple, and when his hands touched them, he cried to GOD and down came the building on thousands of Philistines. You can slay more spiritual Philistines in the death of your flesh than you can in maintaining it.

We sing, "LORD, send Thy power again. In Thy promise, we believe. LORD, send thy power again." This kind of singing is good, but singing won't bring such power. The crucified life is the only life that can be trusted with His power.

With the awful sense, let us say, "LORD, we have failed You; we can take no glory," (and there is nothing in which we can glory) "but, LORD, let Your power come again, that Your name may be glorified." GOD will answer that kind of a prayer. He will answer the faith of the crucified life that declares, "At any cost, LORD, let Your name be glorified in me."

Beloved, obey the SPIRIT's call to die, to lay down your life for His glory. Live the true life of faith by living the crucified life.

COMPILED ARTICLES

Chapter 1

"Faith," *The Elim Pentecostal Herald*, vol. IV, no. 20 (August 1934): 2-3.

"GOD's Ways," *The Elim Pentecostal Herald*, vol. IV, no. 22 (October 1934): 3-4.

"The Working of Faith Within," *The Elim Pentecostal Herald*, vol. XVIII, no. 190 (February 1948): 16-17, 19.

"GOD Answers Faith," *The Elim Pentecostal Herald*, vol. XVIII, no. 196 (September 1948): 3-5.

Chapter 2

"Some Hindrances to a Life of Faith," *The Elim Pentecostal Herald*, vol. I, no. 3 (July 1931): 1-2.

"Faith," *The Elim Pentecostal Herald*, vol. IV, no. 20 (August 1934): 2-3.

"GOD's Ways," *The Elim Pentecostal Herald*, vol. IV, no. 22 (October 1934): 3-4.

"GOD Answers Faith," *The Elim Pentecostal Herald*, vol. XVIII, no. 196 (September 1948): 3-5.

Chapter 3

"Faith," *The Elim Pentecostal Herald*, vol. IV, no. 20 (August 1934): 2-3.

"GOD's Ways," *The Elim Pentecostal Herald*, vol. IV, no. 22 (October 1934): 3-4.

"The Way to GOD," *The Elim Pentecostal Herald*, vol. VI, no. 41 (August 1936): 1, 6.

"GOD Answers Faith," *The Elim Pentecostal Herald*, vol. XVIII, no. 196 (September 1948): 3-5.

Chapter 4

"The Red Heifer," *The Elim Pentecostal Herald*, vol. XIII, no. 115 (June 1943): 1-2.

Chapter 5

"Calvary," *The Elim Pentecostal Herald*, vol. VII, no. 50 (May 1937): 5.

"The LORD Reigneth from the Tree," *The Elim Pentecostal Herald* (June 1959): 8-9.

Chapter 6

"How Faith Works," *The Elim Pentecostal Herald*, vol. XVI, no. 175
(October 1946): 8-9.

"Cause and Effect of Gethsemane," *The Elim Pentecostal Herald*, vol.
XVIII, no. 192 (April 1948): 2-4.

"GOD Answers Faith," *The Elim Pentecostal Herald*, vol. XVIII, no. 196
(September 1948): 3-5.

Chapter 7

"Faith Principles," *The Elim Pentecostal Herald*, vol. XVI, no. 170 (April
1946): 8-9.

"The Working of Faith Within," *The Elim Pentecostal Herald*, vol. XVIII,
no. 190 (February 1948): 16-17, 19.

"A Right Confession," *The Elim Pentecostal Herald*, vol. XVIII, no. 195
(August 1948): 16-19.

Chapter 8

"GOD'S Presence with Us," *The Messenger*, yearbook (1946): 35.

"As I was with Moses . . . ," *The Elim Pentecostal Herald* (April 1955):
10-11, 15.

Chapter 9

"The Life of Faith," *The Elim Pentecostal Herald*, vol. VI, no. 43 (October
1936): 1, 12.

"Accursed—Devoted," *The Elim Pentecostal Herald*, vol. XIX, No. 202
(March 1949): 6-7.

"Through His Poverty," *The Elim Pentecostal Herald*, vol. XXIV, no. 230
(March-April 1952): 8-9.

Chapter 10

"The Crucified Life," *The Elim Pentecostal Herald*, vol. IV, no. 14
(January 1934): 3, 12.

"The Crucified Life," *The Elim Pentecostal Herald*, vol. VI, no. 42
(September 1936): 1.

"Brother Spencer's Admonition," *The Apprehender*, yearbook (1942): 12-13.

GENERAL INDEX

SCRIPTURAL INDEX

MORE ABOUT THE AUTHOR

Ivan Quay Spencer was born November 28, 1888, to home-steaders in the Allegheny foothills of northern Pennsylvania. The second son of Merritt and Alice Spencer seemed destined to farm the family's 160 acres. But stories of early days of Methodism told to the small congregation in the West Franklin Methodist Church gripped young Ivan with a desperate hunger to know and experience GOD for himself. As he later said, "The calling of GOD is not necessarily to be a minister or a missionary, but the call of GOD for you is unto GOD Himself."

In response to that call, Ivan left the farm in 1909 to attend Wyoming Seminary in Pennsylvania. After just one semester there, he had to return home for he was very ill with typhoid. Discouraged and sick on the train ride home, he heard GOD say, "Don't be discouraged. I will heal you if you'll trust in Me." Ivan affirmed his trust in GOD, went to sleep, and awoke well. From that moment on, he believed in Divine healing, preached it, and saw evidence of it in his ministry.

Ivan received his training for ministry from Rochester Bible Training School (RBTS) in Rochester, New York. It was an important center of early Pentecostalism, its populace having received the Pentecostal outpouring of the HOLY SPIRIT in the summer of 1907—just on the heels of Azusa Street. Ivan enrolled in the fall of 1911 and received his personal Pentecost the following year. It was during his time at RBTS that he received a vision of large flaming red letters spelling "REVIVAL." In that moment, he knew he had been commissioned to revival ministry.

Also while at RBTS, Ivan fell in love with Minnie Back, a faithful face at Elim Tabernacle, the school's church. Upon his graduation from RBTS in 1913, the two were married and began ministry together conducting evangelistic meetings while Ivan continued to farm for their livelihood. In 1920, he pioneered a church in Hornell, New York, and then moved on to Endicott, New York.

In 1924, while pastoring in Endicott, GOD spoke to Ivan to open a training school to train young men and women for last days' revival ministry. Elim Bible Institute was the result. As graduates left Elim and pursued national and international ministry, a ministerial fellowship was formed in 1932 to commission and credential graduates. Elim Fellowship thus was birthed.

Ivan attended the constitutional convention of the National Association of Evangelicals (NAE) in May of 1943. He also served on the board of administration for the Pentecostal Fellowship of North America from its inception in 1948. He was first licensed with the Methodist Episcopal Church and later credentialed by the Assemblies of God, all before founding Elim Bible Institute and Elim Fellowship.

On August 17, 1970, Ivan Q. Spencer received the reward of one who lived the life of faith—eternity with the FATHER. For more information, see *Ivan Spencer: Willow in the Wind* by Marion Meloon which chronicles his life of faith.

ABOUT THE EDITOR

Edie Mourey is an author and freelance editor with special interest in Charismatic/Pentecostal texts. Her first book, *Elim: Living in the Flow*, was published by Elim Bible Institute and Elim Fellowship in 1999. She edits and writes in New York's Southern Tier where she, her husband, and daughter reside. You may contact her at edit@furrowpress.com.

Order Form

You may order copies of *Faith: Living the Crucified Life* either by mail or online.

Order by Mail

To place your order, please complete the information below, tear out this form, and mail the form and your check or money order to:

Furrow Press
P.O. Box 98
Big Flats, NY 14814-0098

Name: _____

Street Address: _____

City: _____ State: _____ Zip: _____

E-mail: _____

QTY.	x PRICE	= TOTAL
_____	$12.95 ea.	$ _____
NY Residents add 8% Sales Tax		$ _____
Shipping		$ ___4.60___
Total Enclosed (U.S. funds only)		$ _____

Quantities of 1-4 books are shipped US Priority Mail®.
Quantities of 5 or more are shipped US Media Mail®.

Order Online

Visit our Web site at www.furrowpress.com for credit card orders and quantity discounts.

FURROW
P R E S S